ESTD 1815

"Upon due arrival at West Tarbert we boarded the steamer bound for Port Ellen, a journey occupying some hours, yet withal rendered pleasant by weather that was all that could be desired. Tired and hungry after our long day we were glad to reach our destination and immediately on landing proceeded to the White Hart Inn...The next morning we were early astir exploring the town and sea-shore, after which we partook of a substantial breakfast and started on our way to Ardbeg, distant four miles. The road mostly followed the coast line, but frequently a turn brought us almost to the water's edge. The shore is mostly rocky and dangerous, in many places huge masses of rock rise from the surface of the sea, forming tiny islets round and over which the swell rises and falls in impressive grandeur. Every now and then as we drove along, the scene assumed a new aspect; now we would come suddenly upon some little picturesque bay fringed with fantastic and peculiar shaped rocks, or ascending a gentle hill some inland view of green slopes and heather covered hills would reveal itself, which lent a happy contrast to the wild sea-girt shore...Journeying along we were continually reminded by the ruins of castles and churches that we were on one of the most historic islands of Scotland, in the land of romance and the home of the Lord of the Isles, rendered classic by one of Sir Walter Scott's finest poems.

As we reached the top of a hill, a sudden view of beautiful Ardbeg, presented itself to view and recalled our minds from romantic wanderings. The Ardbeg Distillery is situated on the south-east coast of the island, in a lonely spot on the very edge of the sea, and its isolation tends to heighten the romantic sense of its position."

Alfred Bernard, extract from The Whisky Distilleries of the United Kingdom 1887

The road to Ardbeg

Dunyvaig Castle
Home to the Lord of the Isles

Preface by Gavin D Smith

Today, single malt whiskies from the Hebridean island of Islay are arguably the most desirable in the world. Not too many years ago the vast proportion of spirit made by Islay's distilleries found its way into blended whiskies, but the single malt revolution of the 1980s and '90s saw the 'whisky island's characterful and individualistic drams gain international recognition among connoisseurs, and greater numbers of drinkers have subsequently been drawn to their distinctive charms.

At the time of writing, Islay boasts eight productive distilleries, mostly working at full capacity, while a new plant at Port Charlotte is due on stream in the not too distant future. The buoyant state of the Islay whisky industry mirrors a growing global thirst for Scotch whisky, and at the forefront of Islay's timely 'boom' is a historical distillery which stands proudly on the southern 'Kildalton' shores of the island. Its name is Ardbeg.

Foreword by Graeme Wallace

A simple sip of Ardbeg immediately conjures up images of a bygone era. One taste, or even smell, unravels almost 200 years of hard toil, turbulence, dedication, ambition, passion and an unrelenting story of struggle for survival. Whisky making has survived better in Scotland than in any other country and Ardbeg must surely stand as one of the most traditional and defiant of all Scotch whiskies. Beating the odds and continually bucking the trend, Ardbeg remained largely in production and in private hands for over 120 years while other distilleries faced long period of closure and changing ownership with differing fortunes.

This book chronicles the history, success, closure, near extinction and the remarkable resurgence of Ardbeg distillery. It is a tribute to everyone who has believed in Ardbeg and who has dedicated so much to its survival, resulting in its current status as one of the world's most iconic single malt Scotch whiskies and one of a very few that enjoy a cult following. So pour yourself a dram of Ardbeg and take time to absorb the craftsmanship of the truly unique malt to which this book pays tribute.

Old cask staves

Design – Kevin Jeffery
Printing – Printer Trento, Italy

Published by GW Publishing
PO Box 6091
Thatcham Berks
RG19 8XZ.

Tel + 44 (0)1635 268080
www.gwpublishing.com

ISBN 978-0-9554145-6-5

First published in Great Britain 2008

11 CHALLENGING BEGINNINGS

21 WARS AND PROHIBITION

33 THE GOOD YEARS

45 A PERIOD OF EXPERIMENTATION
AND CLOSURE

59 THE GLENMORANGIE YEARS

75 THE WHISKY MAKERS

95 MAKING THE SPIRIT

137 THE BRAND

159 THE EXPERIENCE

181 SAMPLING THE SPIRIT

195 COLLECTING ARDBEG

The 'new' road into the distillery

CHALLENGING
BEGINNINGS
1815–1902

CHAPTER ONE
PART ONE

ALEXANDER
MACDOUGALL & CO

Ardbeg Distillery in 1886

Inevitably, the history of Ardbeg distillery is inextricably linked with the overall development of Scottish distilling, and it is therefore informative to look at Ardbeg within the wider context of events beyond the shores of Islay.

It was against this backdrop that, in 1815, John MacDougall of Ardbeg decided to become a legitimate, commercial distiller

By the late 18th century whisky making had become commonplace throughout Scotland, both legally and without benefit of licence. Ironically, the whisky being produced by illicit distillers was often of a higher quality than much of the legal 'make,' and was frequently the standard to which the legitimate industry aspired. High levels of duty only served to stimulate the illegal trade.

Islay was no stranger to illicit distilling, which was hardly surprising, considering that the island's first excise officer was not appointed until 1797, a century and a half after excise duty was initially levied on Scotch whisky! By that time, however, a commercial distilling industry was beginning to emerge on Islay. Its development during the next half century owed much to the encouragement received from various members of the Campbell family, who were 'improving' lairds of Islay, until their estates were sold off after Walter Frederick Campbell was sequestrated in 1847. The Campbell dynasty on Islay began with Daniel Campbell, who established the town of Bowmore during the 1760s, and possibly the island's first legal distillery in 1779. South-east of Bowmore, on the rugged, southern 'Kildalton' coastline, there were many stories of distilling taking place in the area of Ardbeg, the most

notable being the 'non-commercial' distilling activities from around 1794 of the MacDougall family, tenants of Ardbeg, Airigh nam Beist and Lagavulin farms.

By the time that Napoleon Bonaparte was defeated at the Battle of Waterloo in June 1815, Britain as a whole was suffering from economic depression, partly caused by the lengthy Napoleonic Wars fought against France. Adverse economic conditions were compounded by more than a decade of extreme weather and famine in some parts of Britain, while on the distilling front there had been notable increases in duty to help finance the war and periods when whisky-making was banned in order to preserve the meagre cereal crops available to feed the people. New legislation ensured that speed of distillation was financially advantageous to distillers, at the expense of quality, and there was a predictable increase in illicit distillation.

There were also concerted attempts to suppress the smuggling trade, and it was against this backdrop that, in 1815, John MacDougall of Ardbeg decided to become a legitimate, commercial distiller, backed by Glasgow whisky merchant Thomas Buchanan Jnr. The following year, Walter Frederick Campbell took over the family's Islay estates, and played a significant part in stimulating the island's distilling industry, most notably by establishing a steamer service between Port Ellen and Glasgow, via Loch Fyne.

1816 not only saw Campbell take up the reins of the Islay estates, but in the same year duty levels were reduced in an effort to encourage legal distilling in Scotland. Additionally, the Small Stills Act removed the fiscal differences between Highland and Lowland distilling on either side of the theoretical Highland Line, as well as allowing the use of stills with a minimum capacity of 40 gallons. These measures had the effect of stimulating Scotch whisky distilling generally, and Islay was no exception, with Lagavulin and the now lost distilleries of Ardmore, Ballygrant, Bridgend, Octovullin, Octomore, Newton and Scarabus all being established – or legalised - soon after the Small Stills Act came into effect.

The 1822 Illicit Distillation Act and the subsequent 1823 Excise Act also made the future appear promising for legal whisky-making operations. The 1823 Act broke the near monopoly enjoyed by large, Lowland distillers and opened the English market to the Highlanders. Duty was halved and legal producers could viably increase the quality of their whisky. On Islay, the 1823 Excise Act encouraged the creation of Lossit, Mulindry, Glenavullen, Port Ellen and Lochindaal distilleries, while Ardbeg became the largest distillery on the island, with an output of 500 gallons per week (65,000 litres per annum) by 1835.

However, the story of the Scotch whisky industry has never been straightforward or predictable and this period of promise was short lived. Although Ardbeg enjoyed a plentiful supply of locally grown barley and had comparatively good access to markets on the mainland, there was a growing problem of surplus whisky stocks throughout the industry. By the 1840s, the Scottish Lowland distillers were benefiting from cheap fuel and improved transportation, making it more difficult once again for the Highland distilleries to compete.

This resulted in a dramatic fall in the overall number of distilleries operating in Scotland, but Ardbeg was one of the survivors, and some 20 years after its formal establishment, the distillery was being run by John MacDougall's son, Alexander, a 'stout and loyal clansman' who had changed the business name to Alexander MacDougall & Co by 1838. Within twelve years, the day to day management had become the responsibility of Charles Hay, son of the laird Walter Frederick Campbell's coachman.

While consumption of whisky in England grew through the 1850s, it was principally the Lowland distillers who benefited. The Highland distillers' market was predominantly in Scotland, where consumption had fallen by 25 per cent, largely due to successful temperance campaigns and a sluggish economy. Despite Islay and Campbeltown whiskies commanding a higher price than many others, the number of distilleries on Islay had fallen from 28 to 16 by 1854, reflecting the situation throughout the Highlands and islands.

Traditionally, most whisky was sold and consumed straight from the still, and did not enjoyed the luxury of maturation in wooden casks

The following year, duty was raised again and malt duty and drawback (the rebate of some tax paid by producers) were abolished. Excise duty between England and Scotland was also equalised, and the existing difference now disappeared. These measures had the effect of causing more hardship for many of the smaller Highland distillers. Ardbeg was far from immune to these problems, and by 1857 the business was making heavy losses. It had been owned by Alexander MacDougall's sisters, Margaret and Flora since 1851, and as a result of the losses incurred they had little option but to sell the distillery to their financial backer and fellow partner, Thomas Gray Buchanan. During the next decade, the steady decline in the number of distilleries continued, as did the consumption of whisky in both England and Scotland.

Traditionally, most whisky was sold and consumed straight from the still, and did not enjoy the luxury of maturation in wooden casks. This resulted in considerable inconsistency at best, but under the provisions of the Forbes Mackenzie Act of 1853 vatting of malt whiskies from the same distillery while 'under bond' was permitted by law for the first time, resulting in a more consistent product. Seven years later, William Gladstone's Spirits Act went a radical stage further, by allowing malts and grains 'under bond' to be blended for the first time, and together these two pieces of legislation were to have far reaching affects on the future of the Scotch whisky industry

Blending malt and grain whiskies produced a more consistent product than had previously been available, and it was also less assertive and more suited to a wider range of palates than most malt whisky. Consequently, the 1860s proved a boom time for whisky distillers, and by the end of the decade production was at an all time high. Although blended whisky was becoming popular, 'self' whiskies, as single malts were usually known, began to benefit from periods of maturation sometimes in excess of five years, and often in former Sherry casks, which helped to give them a more rounded and mellow character.

At Ardbeg, Colin Hay, son of Charles, had taken over the running of the distillery and was made a partner in the business with Thomas Gray Buchanan's son, Alexander Wilson Buchanan, in September 1872. Five years later Scotch whisky output was running at a record level. Islay malts were highly prized by the blenders as their strong character allowed them to use a higher percentage of grain whisky, which was considerably cheaper than malt spirit. Ardbeg was particularly sought after and in 1879 the merchant James Fleming of Glasgow stated that "I will blend your cask and some old Campbeltown together and hope to send you a superior article."

Due to the popularity of Ardbeg for blending, and perhaps because it was owned by a blending company, its proprietors appear to have neglected its promotion as a single malt, even in rapidly developing markets such as Australia and South Africa, where Islay whiskies were particularly appreciated. During this period, various whisky associations were established, including a society for Islay distilleries, and in 1877 the Distillers Company Limited (DCL) was formed, while numerous new distilleries were also built. These included Bruichladdich and Bunnahabhain, which were founded on Islay in 1881.

With four floor maltings in operation and a work force of 60 people, Ardbeg continued to have a higher level of output than any other Islay distillery

1884 brought another economic depression, and as a consequence more amalgamations and takeovers took place within the whisky industry. Numerous Islay distilleries were acquired by major firms in order to guarantee supplies of malt for blending purposes, but Ardbeg remained staunchly independent. Despite the difficulties of this time, Ardbeg was producing

250,000 proof gallons when Alfred Barnard visited the distillery in 1886. With four floor maltings in operation and a work force of 60 people, Ardbeg continued to have a higher level of output than any other Islay distillery

Ardbeg was commanding one of the highest prices for its spirit

In 1888 Alexander Wilson Buchanan and Colin Hay signed a new lease for Ardbeg Farm with John Ramsay. This document was witnessed by David Campbell Lawson, an employee of the Gray Buchanan's company. In time, his family would become major players in Ardbeg's history. Ramsay was the dynamic former business partner of Walter Frederick Campbell, and licence-holder at Port Ellen distillery from 1836. He had acquired the Kildalton section of the former Campbell estates in 1855, thereby becoming the owner of several Islay distilleries.

The 1890s were one of the greatest boom eras ever experienced by the Scotch whisky industry, and Ardbeg was commanding one of the highest prices for its spirit. Plans were drawn up for a railway line to run from the pier to the distillery, although this never materialised. More distilleries were being constructed and output increased, though the eventual outcome was to be another bout of over-supply, and a serious recession. While the good times lasted, export markets for Scotch whisky were being enthusiastically developed in the USA, South America and Germany, and at the same time bases were being set up in the more established colonial countries of Australia and South Africa.

Throughout this period, Colin Hay appears to have done a good job of running the distillery and had established a commendable reputation

as a decent and generous man. He did much for the thriving and close-knit village community of around 200 people, complete with a school, shops and even a choir. His sister had married into the MacDougall clan and her son would later manage Ardbeg for a period, restoring the MacDougall's direct involvement with Ardbeg, albeit for a comparatively short time.

Alas, the success of the Victorian heyday for Scotch whisky peeked in 1900, ushering in the decline which started another long period of instability. Faced with an uncertain future, many companies looked to The Distillers Company Ltd for support, and this support often took the form of DCL acquiring shares or entire companies during the next few decades. Many of the distilleries purchased by DCL were subsequently closed down, bringing criticism from some quarters, though others recognised DCLs ability to anticipate future demand for whisky and produce spirit in line with that demand, thereby safeguarding the longer term interests of the industry.

The latter years of the 19th century had already seen Islay malts falling out of favour with some blenders and being replaced by mellower and more floral Speysides, and the shift away from the heavier style of whiskies to smoother blends using malt from Speyside continued. It was during these troubled and changing times that due to poor health Colin Hay resigned his part of the partnership to his two sons, Walter and Colin Elliot Hay, and to David Lawson, in 1896. Colin Elliot Hay took over the day to day running of the distillery in 1904, but he already had a reputation as a weak man who had grown up living off his father's good nature and success.

Ardbeg Distillery from the southwest, c1910 The distillery appears in full production and in pristine condition. The large house on the shore was built for distillery manager Colin Hay. Note there are no windows in the lower part of the house

ARDBEG, ISLAY.

Loading the SS Clydesdale at Ardbeg Pier. Mr Alex Campbell (distillery manager 1900–1914) can be seen smoking a pipe while supervising the workers

Excerpt from "Export Guardian," December 1912.

A Famous Highland Distillery.

An Ideal Site and an Ideal Product.

THE reputation which Scotland has so long held for the manufacture of high-class whisky to a certain extent hinders our friends overseas from realising the care and skill which are exercised in the preparation and distribution of the national beverage. The habit of association has done not a little to imbue unthinking minds with the vague idea that Scotch whisky is almost as natural to the country as Scotch mist. That this is far from being the case is made very evident by taking a tour through one of our modern distilleries. For instance, let us go to the famous Ardbeg Distillery and see there what are the conditions under which whisky is made, and in some degree we will realise how it is that there is no whisky in the world to compare with that which comes from the

"LAND OF BROWN HEATH AND SHAGGY WOOD."

It is in the romantic and beautiful island of Islay that we find Ardbeg Distillery, situated in a sweet secluded spot close to the verge of the great Atlantic Ocean. Over these broad waters come the invigorating breezes which give the countryside that fresh and healthy atmosphere which makes the landscape stand out in such clear and bold relief. In front of Ardbeg the sea is studded with many rocks, making the coast dangerous to the inexperienced pilot, but near the land is a fine bay providing a safe and pleasant anchorage. The making of whisky is no new thing in this district, for long before the time of the vigilant Excise authorities and licensed trading the place was noted for its whisky, and in later times the smuggler and illicit distiller haunted the caves and glens of the neighbourhood.

The passing of those wild days brought a change, and nearly one hundred years ago a distillery was founded at Ardbeg. This was in the year 1815, and the founders were the MacDougalls of Ardbeg, an old Islay family, the last survivor of whom was Alexander MacDougall, whose name, as a good Highland representative one, is still retained in the firm.

All the distillery workers, and those on Ardbeg Farm, connected therewith, are comfortably housed, and form a little village of about 150 inhabitants. There is a good school close to the village, and with an ample water supply the comfort, cleanliness, and general wellbeing of the inhabitants has always been a notable feature. Most of the employees have been born and bred about the place, and naturally take a keen interest in the welfare of Ardbeg and all matters connected with the advancement of the district.

In the olden days all the Islay distilleries were small, and seventy years ago Ardbeg, though among the larger works, had only a capacity of about six hundred gallons per week, and since that time it has increased more than tenfold—a proof of its high appreciation by blenders and the Trade generally. The water used in distilling, etc., is obtained from two lochs, situated some three miles above their works among heathery hills, and runs over rocky cascades and through peat mosses till uncontaminated it falls into the distillery reservoir.

The pure peaty softness of the water is admirably adapted for distilling purposes, and, doubtless, helps to give the whisky its recognised character and flavour. Finest Scotch barley (malted and entirely kiln-dried with peat on the premises) is alone used in manufacturing the product. A large quantity of peat is required annually, and from May onwards till the month of August considerable labour and expense are incurred in cutting, drying, and storing the peats, which are of a specially good quality for malt drying, being free from sulphur or other offensive mineral, and have for many years back been cut from the same mosses.

With the expansion of the demand for "Ardbeg," the entire buildings and plant have from time to time been added to, improved and renovated, so that in labour-saving and other machinery, management, and storage of malt, drying of draff, warehouse accommodation, etc., the distillery, with its electric light throughout, compares favourably with the most modern equipped work of the kind. The warehouses (eight in number) have storage room for over 17,000 casks of various sizes, equal to 1,002,000 gallons. There is a quay of well-built masonry about six hundred yards from works, at which vessels of large tonnage can load and unload whisky and other goods, and at which MacBrayne's goods steamer makes a weekly call. This quay was erected some thirty years ago almost entirely at the firm's expense.

The present plant is capable of producing over 6000 bulk gallons a week. "Ardbeg," on account of its high quality, characteristic flavour, softness and bouquet, commands the highest price of the "Islay Malts," and for its "covering" and other properties is much in request by blenders, being extensively used in most of the higher class brands now on the market. Among connoisseurs, who have acquired a taste for a single distinctive flavoured malt whisky, "Ardbeg" is considered to be at its best about eight years old.

To suit family arrangements, the firm was converted into a private limited company over ten years ago. The firm are distillers from malt only, not dealers or merchants otherwise. Mr. Colin E. Hay, son of the late managing partner, Mr. Colin Hay (who for over fifty years resided and managed at Ardbeg), is chairman and managing director of the company and is also resident there, supervising the practical work of manufacture.

The controlling agents for sale of "Ardbeg" (United Kingdom and foreign) are Buchanan, Wilson & Co., Ltd., 162 St. Vincent Street, Glasgow, which firm have been closely connected with and have held the sole agency for "Ardbeg" for the last seventy five years.

From the fine half-tone illustrations which have been supplied to us through the courtesy of the firm, a good idea may be got not only of the splendid buildings and their equipment, but also of the various processes of manufacture which the whisky has to pass through ere it is sent to the markets where it continues to maintain that high reputation for excellence of quality which has since the earliest days been associated with the products of Ardbeg Distillery.

Excerpt from the Export Guardian, December 1912

WARS AND PROHIBITION
1902–1958

CHAPTER ONE
PART TWO

ALEXANDER MACDOUGALL & CO LTD

Colin E Hay c 1920

By 1902, there were at least 40 homes at Ardbeg with "most of the employees having been born and bred about the place." In July of that year, Alexander MacDougall & Co became a limited company. The company's shares were owned by two members of the Hay family, two members of the Gray Buchanan family and three members of the Lawson family. While the Gray Buchanans had been financing Ardbeg from the outset and the Hays had been managing the distillery for over 50 years, the Lawson family's association in terms of share ownership only dated from 1896, when David Lawson, originally a clerk with Buchanan, Wilson & Co, took a financial interest in Ardbeg. Ultimately, his niece, Kathleen, was to become the largest individual shareholder in Ardbeg Distillery Ltd.

From 1900 to 1914, long time employee Alex Campbell served as head brewer, effectively running the distillery. During this time a reference was sought for a former member of staff who was seeking work at Clynelish distillery in Sutherland. The reference as supplied read "He left me in temper because I had reason to find fault with him over a small matter and he took it so hot that I had to let him go… I may as well be frank and tell you that he had taken a drop too much the day I challenged him and that is a fault that I am very severe on."

In 1909 Prime Minister David Lloyd George increased the distillers' licence fee, while duty on spirits rose by 3s 9d per proof gallon, taking the retail price of a bottle of whisky above half a crown (12.5p) for the first time. As a devotee of the temperance movement he went on to increase duty year on year, which, predictably, had a major effect on consumption. The situation began to improve between 1911 and 1914, but in the latter year the First World War broke out, and so began a period of severe shortages, restrictions and temporary distillery closures.

Aged in his late 40s, Alex Campbell went off to the war with a number of men from the Kildalton area. Unfortunately, Colin Elliot Hay's weakness as a manager resulted in the loss of Campbell's job while he was away fighting for his country, despite the fact that he had put in more than 34 years of service at Ardbeg. The position was given to Hay's cousin, a MacDougall. (see page 24 for the full story).

In 1915, Lloyd George introduced legislation prohibiting the sale of whisky less than three years old, and two years later there were only eight distilleries still working in Scotland, none of which were producing malt spirit. In 1918, export of whisky was stopped, in order to conserve the meagre stocks available for the home market. The end of the war in 1918 did not bring an end to the difficulties faced by the Scotch whisky industry, however, with the government electing to continue the policy of progressively raising levels of duty. Prohibition was implemented in the USA during 1920, which caused significant hardship for many Scottish distillers, and another decade of economic instability and recession was to follow. Despite still shipping to Canada, Ardbeg distillery suffered as much as anywhere else, and stocks of maturing spirit were low. Interestingly, the distillery received a letter from Laphroaig, complaining that Ardbeg was paying its employees too much compared to the other distilleries on the island!

Ardbeg also received a flurry of letters from private individuals requesting a replenishment of their own supplies (see page 28). Around the same time, the business had been strengthened, with Ardbeg's capital being increased to £40,000, and the distillery and its lands were purchased from John Ramsay for the total sum of £19,000 in 1922. 650 shares in Ardbeg were acquired by the Distillers Company Ltd and James Watson & Co, signifying the start of corporate involvement with Ardbeg. Katherine Lawson's shareholding increased, making her the largest single shareholder, although she appears to have had no direct involvement in the running of the distillery.

In 1928 Colin Elliot Hay died virtually bankrupt, and his 580 Ardbeg shares were sold to Colonel George McNish, in order to settle his debt with the bank. The Colonel was a son of Robert McNish, founder of the Glasgow blenders Robert McNish & Co Ltd, which ultimately became absorbed into the Hiram Walker empire. While the Gray Buchanans remained the major shareholding family in Ardbeg, their shares were largely held by trusts, and the family had little practical involvement, though Janet Edith, Mary Rose and Kate Farie Gray Buchanan did hold shares in their own right. However, the Lawson family's interest was to increase with the passing of 50 shares to Daniel Lawson in 1929. He would eventually become chairman of the board.

Ardbeg was more fortunate than many of its fellow Islay distilleries during the troubled inter-war years, when several closed down. Although most eventually reopened, one permanent casualty was Lochindaal in Port Charlotte, which fell silent in 1929. Production levels at Ardbeg had risen by 1928, but this was at the expense of heavy price cutting and was followed by an economic crisis in 1931. The following

year just three members of staff were on the payroll.

Happily for the Scotch whisky industry, US Prohibition ended in 1933, ushering in a period of optimism and growth, which continued for the rest of the decade. The lifting of Prohibition led the large, Canadian-based Hiram Walker Gooderham & Worts corporation to acquire George Ballantine & Son and two Speyside distilleries; going on to construct their own vast grain distillery at Dumbarton, near Glasgow during 1937/38.

The outbreak of the Second World War in 1939 precipitated the next downturn in Scotch whisky distilling, with barley and coal becoming scarce and taxes once again being raised to help finance the conflict. In 1940 distilling continued at Ardbeg, but output was less than half that of the previous year. Records show, however, that by this time Ardbeg was supplying whisky to The Distillers Agency Ltd, John Haig & Co, John Dewar & Sons, Robert McNish & Co Ltd, William Grant & Sons, Long John Distilleries Ltd and Rutherford & Co. The distillery was also filling for George Ballantine & Son, John Walker & Sons, Stewart & Son of Dundee Ltd and Macdonald & Muir Ltd. The last named company would eventually become outright owners of Ardbeg, changing their name to Glenmorangie plc in 1996.

1941 and 1942 saw the virtual closure of Ardbeg, with the distillery running for just a few weeks of the year, and no whisky at all was produced in 1943. With the cessation of hostilities two years later, Ardbeg's stills were fired up once again, and Prime Minister Winston Churchill's far-sighted acknowledgement that Scotch whisky was a great, dollar-earning export asset heralded a period of tremendous growth, serving to re-establish Scotch whisky as a highly desirable commodity all over the world. Although the US consumed as much whisky as it could obtain, the older colonial countries, such as Australia and South Africa, suffered as a consequence of high import duties.

The British economy was notably weak as a result of the war, despite the crucial foreign currency being earned abroad by whisky, and it was not until 1953 that restrictions on production were fully lifted. Even then, the shortage in maturing stocks meant that normality did not return for some years. Nonetheless, justified optimism was the order of the day, and the Scotch whisky industry embarked on another period of amalgamation and investment, with silent distilleries reopening, existing plants undergoing upgrading and enlargement, and entirely new distilleries being built from scratch.

As the industry began to gear up for the good times, Alexander McDougall & Co, went into liquidation in 1958 and the Ardbeg Distillery Ltd was formed on 5th January 1959. A new chapter in Ardbeg's lengthy history was opening.

Dorothy Dennis is a retired general practitioner who now lives on Islay. Her grandfather was Alexander Campbell, distillery manager at Ardbeg during the early years of the 20th century, when some 40 families were resident there, including the Hays, MacDougalls, and two excise officers.

According to Dorothy, "Alexander Campbell was born in Port Ellen and went to school there. When he left school he went to work in the office at Ardbeg distillery, and by the time the First World War broke out in 1914 he was distillery manager. He was in the territorials, so was called up at the start of the war, and went off with the boys from Kildalton as a captain in the 8th battalion of the Argyll & Sutherland Highlanders.

"Colin Elliot Hay owned Ardbeg at that time, and he promised my grandfather his job back when the war was over. However, Hay was an alcoholic and was dominated by his wife, who gave the job to one of her cousins, known as 'Wee MacDougall.' The manager's house had a window that looked across to the house lived in by the Hays, and Mrs Hay insisted that the window was glazed so that nobody could look out and see into their house! Grandfather's family were turned out of the manager's house and went to Glasgow, like so many Islay folk. There they stayed with relatives and finally got a flat. After the war, grandfather joined them, but he was unemployed for a long time, and finally got a job in the docks as a security man. He died in the 1930s."

Alexander Campbell's son, also Alexander, studied to become a doctor, and returned to Islay in 1928 as a medical officer. Not long before his death in 1998, he recorded some early memories of Islay, and in particular of Ardbeg.

"I was born in Ardbeg on 17 August 1901, in what was then the distillery manager's house, my father being the manager. The house was a somewhat unusual one. It was old and was physically attached to part of the distillery - in fact a wing built out from the stillroom consisting of three storeys. Between the wall of the house and the sea with the wee pier, was a road, and in stormy weather the sea sprayed bits of seaweed onto the windows.

As far as I can remember there was electricity in the house because it was used in the distillery, but it was variable and not always available. It was fitted in the houses of the managing director, the manager, and the two excise officers, and gave light only. The power for the generator was from a water wheel. The water was led in a covered stone built lade from the dam at the top of the village which first supplied a water wheel at the farmhouse threshing mill. The dam in turn was fed by a burn coming from Loch Iarnan, some miles away in the hills and good for trout. We had cold water in the house, but were better off than the distillery workers who had to draw their water from standpipes. Even worse, however, was that while we had a flush lavatory, the only 'conveniences' in the village were horrible, filthy, dry closets. Absolutely disgraceful.

My principal friend was Dougie McIntyre who years later was distillery manager during part of the time when I was GP. The older boys (including me) and some of the girls, got jobs in summer as part of the peat squad, our job being mostly barrowing and spreading the peats out to dry immediately they were cut. Some of the village wives were also employed in this capacity. The gaffer's wife was also one of the squad, and when we stopped work about midday to boil our tea cans and eat our pieces, they both retired to a small hut which stood on the bank above the loch. We could soon hear their snores.

A track led up the hill to a 'bothan' in which lived a man called 'Done' (Duncan McCuaig) with his unmarried sister 'Babby' (Barbara). When I was a boy I thought he was a wild, fierce individual because he used to come to the village occasionally and have a drink of caochan, or wash, which was the crude fermenting liquid before it was distilled into whisky. He used to sneak into the tun room and drink this stuff from a vat. He would then become roaring drunk and stagger off home. I saw him once being elbowed along by my father as he helped to get him quickly on his way home.

On most summer evenings three or four boats would be out from each village fishing till dark. Saithe, lythe and mackerel were the common catches, and when fish were plentiful, some of the catch was shared with old people, widows, or any others unable to fish for themselves."

Ardbeg distillery from the north, c1920, showing the various farm buildings

Letters from the 1920s

'My father is staying with me at present. After subsisting for some years on weak and inferior spirits he craves for some good stuff. Neither he nor I are capitalists so shall be glad if you will send us as soon as possible as small a cask of Ardbeg as you can supply, while at the same time we should like the strength to be as great as possible.'

W Fraser

'I thank you for your offer to send a cask of pre-war quality whisky, and I shall of course not mention it…'

Major Wilkinson

'Kindly make sure that I get your own whisky as I cannot drink these whiskies that are all mixed together. I have been so accustomed to drink your good whisky that I cannot favour any other.'

Hugh MacDiarmid

'I do not know the meaning of a small octave but think it sounds very tempting. Procuring whisky in Edinburgh is literally a hand to mouth business so that I can literally take as much as you can give and I can afford!'

F Graham Robertson

We have absolutely been relying upon you to supply our customary Christmas requirements of whisky and would therefore look upon it as a special favour if you could manage to supply us with say at least 18 to 20 cases.'

Crown Preserved Coal Co, Cardiff

'Dear Archie I have had a very poor new year as I have had pleurisy some time ago and had to stay at home lately and take care of myself and I had no keg of Ardbeg. Please see Colin Hay and talk him nicely to send me a ten gallon cask of old Ardbeg.'

John Blackley

'I spend lots of time every day writing certificates to show that various influenza patients require it (Ardbeg).

Dr Fraser of Chasetown

TELEPHONE No. 5671
CENTRAL

Entd:

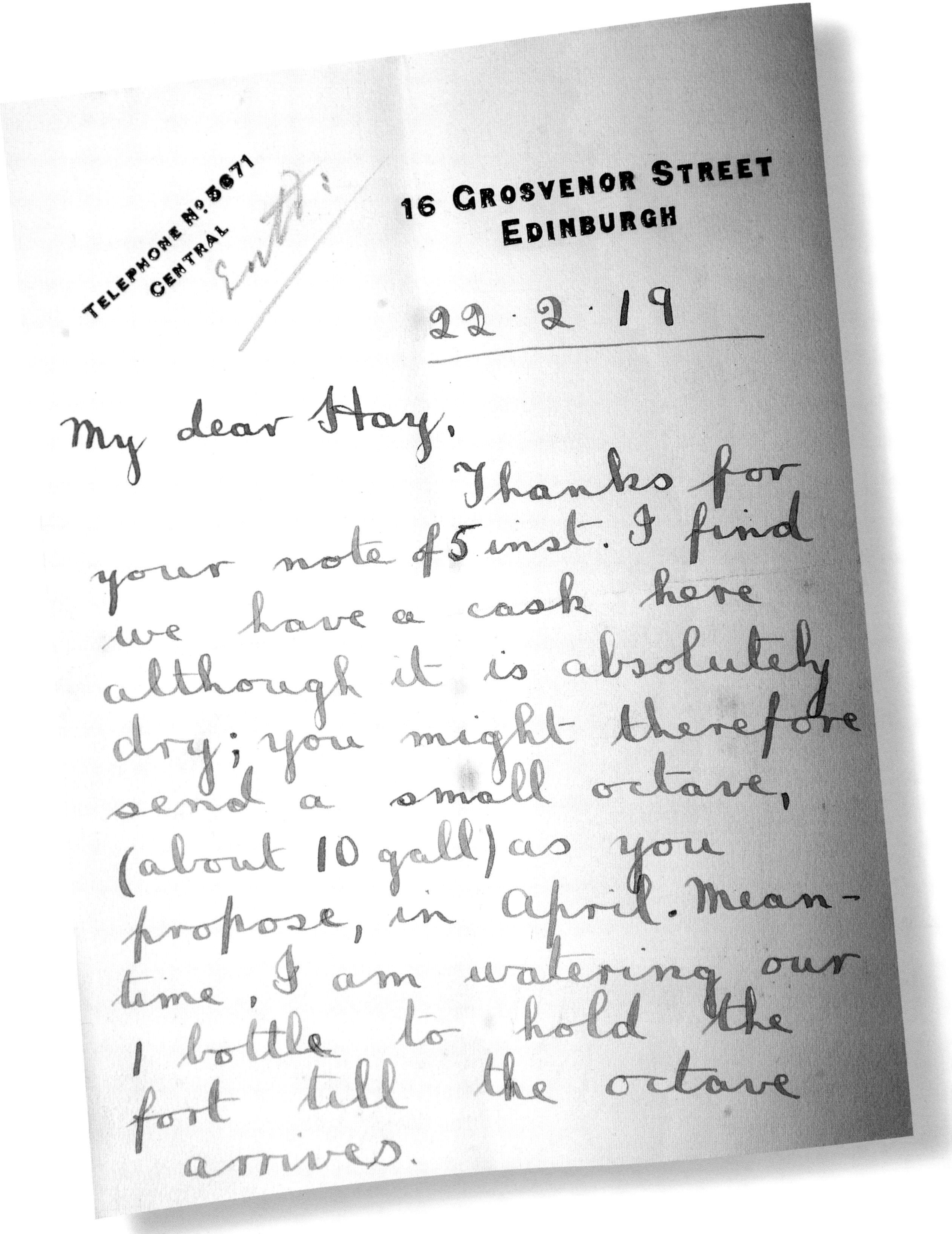

16 GROSVENOR STREET
EDINBURGH

22.2.19

My dear Hay,

Thanks for your note of 5 inst. I find we have a cask here although it is absolutely dry; you might therefore send a small octave, (about 10 gall) as you propose, in April. Meantime, I am watering our 1 bottle to hold the port till the octave arrives.

Cutting peat for Ardbeg and the Ardbeg filling store, c1910

Two views of Ardbeg from the east and from the southwest, c1940. The tall chimneys were knocked down in 1966/7 just after an oil-fired boiler had been installed

Cask stencilling equipment

THE GOOD YEARS
1959-1976

CHAPTER TWO
PART ONE

ARDBEG
DISTILLERY LTD

*Mr MacIntyre (distillery manager 1952-1964) and
Mr Dan Lawson (long time director of the board and chairman 1973-74)*

The creation of Ardbeg Distillery Ltd in January 1959 effectively took the distillery out of private control for the first time in its existence. Both The Distillers Company Ltd (DCL) and Hiram Walker Ltd substantially increased their share in the company, though the major shareholdings remained in private hands. Mr Hugh Cowan-Dougal, representing the Gray Buchanan's interests, and Mr Dan Lawson, representing his family, had seats on the board, along with figures from DCL and Hiram Walker.

A request by Messrs Churtons Ltd to bottle and sell old 'Ardbeg' at home and abroad was considered and agreed by the board, which noted "The label must be approved by us showing the word Ardbeg." It is unclear whether the bottling actually proceeded.

DCL placed an order for 700 casks to be filled each year for three years from 1960, which was a 200 per cent increase on their previous commitment. Despite this, just over 300,000 proof litres was produced in 1959, rising slowly to about 400,000 by 1964. With this vote of confidence by DCL and as part of an increasingly buoyant and expanding Scotch whisky industry, a modernisation programme was implemented in 1962 to increase the efficiency of the distillery. It was also decided to approach selected prospective new customers direct, "sending samples of old and new Ardbeg," rather than spend money on general advertising in monthly trade publications.

This is the first reference ever made to advertising and marketing Ardbeg whisky, though an element of financial caution is clearly evident. In the same year Mr Cowan-Dougal died, bringing to an end any direct involvement in the making of Ardbeg whisky by the Gray Buchanan family, which had financially backed Ardbeg from the outset in 1815. The following year, long time employee and distillery manager Dougie MacIntyre became ill, resulting in his taking early retirement after almost 50 years of service at Ardbeg. Hamish Scott was appointed distillery manager in May 1964, taking up his post on 1 September 1964.

"I started work at Ardbeg soon after finishing my National Service," recalls Hamish. "Prior to my time there, Dougie MacIntyre was manager for around 12 years, and before that Hamish McMurchie (a Campbeltown man). He was there during the war years.

"I had begun in the whisky industry as a trainee at Aberfeldy distillery, where I worked for three years. Then I went to work in the SMD (Scottish Malt Distillers) Laboratory, at Coates Crescent in Edinburgh. After that I spent time at Ord distillery near Inverness as a temporary assistant, and then I was at Benromach.

"I then went out to Guyana to make rum for two years. They had Coffey stills made from wood, driven by steam. But at that time, the political climate in Guyana was changing, with independence, so I decided to come back to Scotland.

"I joined Scottish Grain Distillers, an offshoot of DCL, as they paid twice that of SMD in those days! I was brewer at Caledonian distillery in Edinburgh and at Cameronbridge in Fife. Then I was offered the manager's job at Ardbeg, and on a beautiful May day we flew over to see the distillery. I'd never been to Islay before. The place was sold for me that day.

"I was impressed with the size of the distillery. There were four malting floors working, but I soon became aware that not much money had been spent on the place. Dougie MacIntyre had even straightened out used nails to save the company money!"

The vast majority of Ardbeg spirit being made was used for blending purposes, and Hamish Scott notes "In 1964 we filled one 50 gallon cask per year for single malt. We were using old casks, so it was becoming very woody."

Hamish Scott's arrival coincided with an increasingly upbeat mood in the industry and as filling requests increased, production at Ardbeg was stepped up from six to eight mashes per week in 1965, and a new warehouse (number 10) was to be built at a cost of £34,310.

In any distillery which operated its own maltings, a reliable source of peat was essential, and this was particularly important in a distillery such as Ardbeg, where the malt was heavily peated. In addition to his managerial duties, Hamish Scott became a founder of Islay Peat Developments, using mechanical peat-cutting equipment to harvest peat for Ardbeg and other Islay distilleries. According to Hamish "Even in the '60s it was difficult to find people willing to cut peat." Hamish also notes that "In my time, everything came in by puffer to the big pier at Ardbeg. Grain and coal. Quite a bit of spirit went out by puffer, and also on the *Lochard*, the MacBrayne's cargo boat."

1965 saw profits more than double that recorded in any of the previous six years, and the following year profits were even higher, principally due to a specially negotiated sales of much of the unwanted mature stocks of 'Old Ardbeg' to DCL. By 1967 almost 700,000 proof litres were being produced, with the maltings running close to capacity.

Ardbeg was clearly an attractive asset in a Scotch whisky industry that was beginning to be consolidated into the hands of a smaller number of large companies, and in 1969 the Canadian distilling giant Joseph E Seagram & Sons expressed an interest in buying the distillery, though nothing came of this approach. Virtually all of Seagram's Scotch whisky assets, held through its Chivas Brothers Ltd subsidiary, were situated on Speyside, so an Islay distillery would have provided them with a useful source of peated malt for blending purposes.

The strong focus of Ardbeg on the blending market (primarily through DCL and Hiram Walker) is illustrated by the fact that the Minutes of 21 December 1970 record "It was agreed that 1 case of Ardbeg (bottled) be allowed to the 3 Hotels on the Island each year at Christmas." Hamish Scott recalls "We had it bottled for us and it sold in local hotels."

"John Hopkin was the excise officer in my time. He was a Welshman, and had about 14 cats. A ginger one used to follow him into the office and sat there all day. He retired in 1975. He kept his dram in a Domestos bottle, so nobody knew what he had! Once a week or so he'd give me the warehouse keys and I went and got my share – about a gallon a week. And he would take the same. Locals would take him a lobster in return for a drop of it. But we had visitors to entertain, too. We didn't drink it all ourselves. And we were still dramming – the guys liked to drink the new spirit."

Hamish Scott:

The following year yet another new warehouse (number 11) was constructed to cope with the high level of output being recorded. Fillings orders were favourable for the new distilling season, and it was proposed to reduce the silent season to just the middle of August. Increased production would mean buying in malt, so it was agreed to install new malt bins.

There are signs that the board of Ardbeg Distillery was beginning to consider bottled malt sales in a more serious way, and the Glasgow Bonding Co was approached regarding bottling Old Ardbeg in 1971, and in 1972 it was agreed that a start should be made to building up a stock of older whisky. In line with the decision to retain stocks of maturing whisky for single malt sales, 1,200 gallons of whisky distilled in the spring of 1968 was bottled in April 1972, at just four years of age. This appears to have been the first 'commercial' bottling of Ardbeg.

By the end of 1972, demand still outstripped supply and so consideration was given to outsourcing malt. It was agreed that not more than 12.5 per cent of bought malt could be used without altering the character of Ardbeg, and Hamish Scott was advised to proceed on this basis. Thus 1972 saw the last vintage of 'peaty' Ardbeg made using malt entirely produced in the on-site floor maltings.

In 1973 Dan Lawson became company chairman. Although on the surface all was well at Ardbeg, with demand for the distillery's fillings being strong, behind the scenes there was a degree of 'political' posturing. The company Minutes for 23 November 1973 noted that "Both Mr McCann and Mr Murray [the Board

Ardbeg appears to have once again missed an opportunity to broaden its customer base and develop its markets

representatives of Hiram Walker and DCL respectively] felt they had not been kept fully informed about the increased filling availability in time to take a decision about their own company requirements." They had also rejected a request from Chivas Bros to fill one hundred hogsheads the previous year. Ardbeg appears to have once again missed an opportunity to broaden its customer base and develop its markets.

The November Minutes also recorded that "As there is no cased 'Ardbeg' in bond it was decided that 4 clr Casks (Spring 63, Spring/Aut 64 and Spring 65) be removed to Glasgow for bottling at 80 proof – natural colouring." With expansion still in mind, it was subsequently agreed that "not more than 15 per cent of bought malt should be used in order to retain the existing characteristics of Ardbeg."

1974 saw production peak at 1.1 million litres of spirit, yet despite the apparent prosperity of Ardbeg, the trustees of the Gray Buchanan family intimated that some or all of their holdings of 14,000 shares might be offered for sale, foreshadowing the future direction the company was to take. Hiram Walker indicated they would be willing to buy at £4 per share and DCL noted that they would also consider buying at this price.

Due to a difficulty in cutting peat during bad weather in 1973 delivery to the distillery had been very much reduced and as a result a less heavily peated whisky was produced in 1974. The additional production for 1974 had been achieved without undue trouble although the spirit yield was considered "not satisfactory" due to a bad yield and the increased throughput.

The filling and selling of a single Ardbeg malt was once again discussed, and Gordon & MacPhail & Co was subsequently approached with a view to bottling, marketing and retailing Ardbeg malt whisky. An agreement was not reached with Gordon & MacPhail, and so an approach was made to Messrs JA Mitchell & Co Ltd of Campbeltown. It was noted that the distillery had negligible stock of well matured Ardbeg, "not filled into the best wood and would not give credit to the name Ardbeg. Mitchells at present hold stock of Ardbeg of ages 17 years and downwards and could obtain mature Ardbeg in sufficient quantities to make the operation viable." Interestingly, Ardbeg had just turn down a three year order from JA Mitchell to fill 30 casks, so relations were presumably none too cordial, and needless to say, nothing came of these discussions either.

Rather ominously, however, DCL indicated they would be reducing their fillings of Ardbeg in 1975, and Hiram Walker indicated they would possibly be willing to take this up, depending on the quantity. DCL did indeed reduce its fillings from 2,300 hogsheads to 1,000, (a drop of around 80,000 original proof gallons), in line with a cut back in production at its own distilleries, and as Hiram Walker did not take up the shortfall, Mr Scott was instructed to "cut back production immediately."

In the meantime "Mr Scott reported that the initial reaction to the Ardbeg bottled in July had been encouraging, but it was very difficult to asses what future demand might be. Of the 345 cases of Ardbeg bottled by Strathleven Bonded Warehouses in July, a total of 110 cases had been sold to date." The board agreed to continue bottling Ardbeg on a small scale. Speaking recently, Hamish Scott recalls "We bottled a ten-year-old and sold 90 cases at a catering and licensed trade exhibition in 1975. By the late 1960s we had been managing to get stock laid down, so that was what we were bottling. We got a lot of repeat business. Generally we were filling into ex-Bourbon casks, though DCL supplied Sherry butts and 'hoggies' for us to fill for them."

The seriousness of the downturn in business for Ardbeg was brought home when Hiram Walker reduced their filling order for 1976 to 60,000 from 165,000. On a slightly more positive note, an order for 50 cases of 'Ardbeg' was received that year from Groothandel Van Wees, Amersfoort, Holland, representing the first major export of bottled Ardbeg. "The chairman stated that bottled Ardbeg had always been available to shareholders and local hoteliers on Islay. To promote bottled Ardbeg would require intensive marketing effort and considerable finance to lay down stocks as the present stock of old Ardbeg was not adequate to bottle on a large scale."

The downturn in Ardbeg's fortunes led Major P Fletcher (nephew of Colin Hay and a relatively minor shareholder) to propose the sale of the private shares in Ardbeg to Hiram Walker. He cited an "imbalance" between the interests of the family and trade shareholders, perceiving the distillery to be at the mercy of DCL and Hiram Walker's pricing policy. Major Fletcher had proposed in January of 1976 a "diversification of our customer range" and "the marketing of Ardbeg as a straight Islay Malt of specialist character," something nearby Laphroaig had effectively been doing for more than a century.

At this time, the Gray Buchanan family owned 14,000 shares, the Lawson family 6,200, the Hay (Fletcher) family 4,200, DCL 6,000 and Hiram Walker 6,800 shares. However, most of the Gray

Buchanan shares were owned by a family trust. With substantial investment being needed in the distillery, despite the production increases of the 1960s and early '70s, Kathleen Lawson's stockbrokers considered Ardbeg "a very unmarketable asset." With this advice in mind, and as the 'senior' and largest private shareholder, Kathleen Lawson went along with Major Fletcher and supported the sale of the privately held shares.

Production for 1976 was just over 400,000 proof litres compared to over 1 million two years earlier, and it was recorded that "No further export orders of bottled Ardbeg had been received, otherwise sales remained steady. It was agreed not to bottle any more in the meantime." Signs that Ardbeg whisky was still a desirable commodity, however, came with a steady stream of individual orders and with the statement that "Under pressure from local traders Miniatures had been bottled for distribution and that sales to date had been encouraging." During the last six months of 1976, a 70° proof bottling with a new label was planned and eventually released.

During the turmoil, Hiram Walker approached DCL early in 1976 with a view to purchasing its shares in the distillery. DCL initially declined, but after Hiram Walker acquired the 27,200 private shares in October for £8 each, giving them an 85 per cent stake in the company, DCL agreed to sell its remaining 15 per cent to Hiram Walker in December.

Former Hiram Walker master blender Robert Hicks offers a historical explanation for why Hiram Walker may have wanted to acquire Ardbeg. "Way back in 1936 Harry C Hatch, president of Hiram Walker, came over to Scotland to place an order with DCL for grain whisky. After being kept waiting for an hour and a half for his meeting he got up, walked out, went home and said 'Nobody is going to do that to me again,' and the company subsequently built the huge Dumbarton distillery two years later. From there Hiram Walker developed a policy of self reliance. This may well have been a deciding factor in their buying Ardbeg."

Members of the board with Hamish Scott, c1970.
From the left:
Dan Lawson (Ardbeg board member 1958-1974) died
George Murray, MD Scottish Malt Distillers
(Ardbeg board member 1967-1976)
Tommy Scott, chairman, Hiram Walker
(Ardbeg board member 1958-1971) died
Hamish Scott, distillery manager 1964-1977
J F A Gibson, chairman, Ardbeg & partner, Messrd Whinney Murray
(Ardbeg board member 1958-1973)
It is unfortunate that in the five years leading up to the sale of Ardbeg, two of the original five board members died, one retired and two had previously retired, leaving none of the founding members or major private shareholders on the board

Mr Whyte from the Commercial Union Insurance Company with Hamish Scott in front of the company minibus

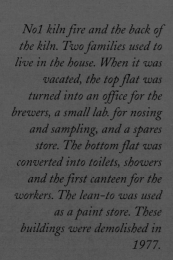

No1 kiln fire and the back of the kiln. Two families used to live in the house. When it was vacated, the top flat was turned into an office for the brewers, a small lab. for nosing and sampling, and a spares store. The bottom flat was converted into toilets, showers and the first canteen for the workers. The lean-to was used as a paint store. These buildings were demolished in 1977.

No1 maltings and the peat store which stood where the visitor car park is located, c1975

No.1 Kiln. Now converted to the Old Kiln Café and Visitor Centre

Old malt barrels

A PERIOD OF EXPERIMENTATION AND CLOSURE
1977-1997

CHAPTER TWO
PART TWO

On 22 December 1976, the company Minutes recorded a transfer of shares, giving Hiram Walker total control of the Ardbeg operation. Six months later Hamish Scott was replaced as manager by Robbie MacArthur, who was responsible for overseeing the renovation of the distillery, including the demolition of some buildings. The house attached to the back of the kiln was removed, as was the warehouse fronting the sea. Robbie McArthur came from Speyside and lived in a caravan during his time at Ardbeg, with just occasional visits from his wife on the mainland. He did not stay on Islay for long.

John Black, who is now manager at Tullibardine distillery, was offered the manager's job at the end of 1977 and visited the island with his family before making a decision. "Now I had never been on Islay before," he says, "and we arrived when it was dark, wet and raining. We went up to the distillery, hung about for a wee while then went up to the hotel at Kildalton. The next day we were away, and that was my first experience at Islay. I just wasn't impressed. My two daughters were also at the wrong age to change schools, so I turned down the job. After that I agreed to go out for four weeks at a time, rotating with two other brewers to support the local man Duncan Logan."

Don Raitt subsequently became manager at Ardbeg, but John Black was considered a valuable asset due to his experience working with floor maltings, having started his distillery career in the maltings at Cardhu distillery on Speyside. "Soon I got used to the place," recalls John, "and was getting to know all the boys, so when I was offered the job to support Don Raitt as assistant manager in 1979, I took it and moved over."

As Hiram Walker's then Group Distilleries Manager Ian Miller recalls, "Until Ardbeg came along our malt distilling operations were centred on Speyside, but Ardbeg was physically far away from that area. The company decided Ardbeg should become my baby, and I first visited it in December 1976, when I had been appointed Group Distilleries Manager. I was responsible for the operation of the distillery and for getting the renovation project up and running and I generally went over about once a month after that. When we acquired it, the place was in a very poor physical condition, and while we demolished some buildings, we also spent a lot of money elsewhere, including in the maltings which were in a very poor state, and on wiring and various electrical items.

"By the time Hiram Walker took over, a number of the old buildings had already been demolished – some of them were not much better than hovels. If Hiram Walker hadn't taken it on the distillery would probably have closed and crumbled away. In the maltings, a lot of the timber was rotten and I don't know what exactly kept the floors up! We spent around £1 million on the distillery, so Hiram Walker was serious about Ardbeg, though the whisky was certainly only seen as a component of a blend for them.

"We ran both sides of the maltings, and they were producing a very heavily-peated malt. It went into the McNish blend and various others, as well as Ballantine's. It was not seen as a single malt at all, but then at that time single malts were not very important to the industry as a whole. Hiram Walker was a 'blends' company and from 1970 they had set about establishing a good distributor network and a strong marketing programme into Europe for Ballantine's. This effort enabled Ballantine's to become a major brand, and in using Ardbeg as a key component, Ardbeg's fortunes became dependent upon that of Ballantine's."

John Black recalls that "Some of the buildings were very run down, and rough, rough, rough! We spent a lot of money on the distillery, replacing the wooden washbacks and copper piping. In 1980 we put a new oil tank into the building with 'Ardbeg' painted on it and removed the old tank. It was taken away to Glasgow just as it was, un-emptied and hanging so far off the back of the lorry.

"One thing we did try was to peat moist malt that had been malted elsewhere, but it did not infuse because it was too late in the process. There was a good atmosphere at Ardbeg with mostly young fellas working the malting floors. They used to have great fun seeing who could have the best section or could turn the malt the quickest. After the men had done the filling of the casks and stowed them, they got a dram. I remember one shift worker who lived in the big house was awoken by his wife to join the back of the queue to get a dram. He claimed a dram even though he had not done the work, then went back to bed! Seems his wife couldn't bear to see him miss out on a free dram."

Soon, Ardbeg was at the centre of a unique experiment with peating levels, as former Hiram Walker master blender Robert Hicks explains. "When Hiram Walker took 100 per cent control of Ardbeg we had rather more capacity there than we could really use, and it was decided to do something different with it. We owned Robert Kilgour's maltsters in Kirkcaldy, and from 1978 to 1981 we sent over plain malt and ran both plain and peated batches of Ardbeg. The unpeated spirit was called Kildalton, and it developed into an Islay malt that you could use as a 'normal' whisky for blending purposes." (See Chapter Six.)

The recently released 10-year-old bottling labelled at 70 proof was changed in 1978 but this too was short-lived due to consumers' apparent difficulty in appreciating the challenging malt.

Consequently the maltings and distillery closed on the 25th March 1981

Despite the innovation of producing Kildalton in addition to 'regular' Ardbeg, Hiram Walker had not owned Ardbeg for long before the Scotch whisky industry as a whole began to feel serious repercussions from the years of over-production in which it had indulged.

Consequently, the maltings and distillery were closed on the 25th March 1981, with Hiram Walker holding a large amount of Ardbeg stock that had to be 'managed out.' As Ian Miller points out, "It wasn't a whisky you could use a lot of in a blend." After 166 years of continuous production, apart from the enforced closures during the war years, Ardbeg fell silent, and few expected that the distillery would ever commence production again.

According to John Black, "at the end of each day we used to sit down and have a dram of Ardbeg. It was a nice place to sit and discuss the day's work for half an hour, but all that's changed now. I was quite sad to see it shut down. Having knocked down some of the derelict building in 1977 the place was looking really nice." Later, in 1981, the big, old house by the shore was demolished which by then was in a very bad state. For some unknown reason the four warehouses behind the big house were also demolished with the tiles and fine, heavy roof timbers and even the corrugated iron being cannibalised and sold off.

Hiram Walker had been a cash-rich company which had previously embarked on an ongoing programme of acquisition. Around 1980 however, they were faced with a hostile takeover of their own and so decided to merge with the Home Oil Company and the Consumers Gas Company - major suppliers of oil and gas to Canada. This resulted in 71 per cent of its commercial interests being in oil and gas and the remaining 29 per cent in distilled spirits.

Due to falling oil prices in 1981, the company was forced to make some valuation write downs and tried to reduce debit. No doubt Ardbeg's closure was part of this process. In 1986 Gulf Canada, owned by the Reichmann family, attempted to acquire Hiram Walker. As they were only interested in the oil-related side of the business, the Reichmann's approached Seagram & Sons Ltd to buy the drinks operation. Hiram Walker therefore agreed to sell its liquor division to Allied–Lyons plc in order to raise cash to fight the takeover. The whole affair was complex and acrimonious, and Allied did not take control until 1987.

Ardbeg was to remain closed until October 1989; two years after Hiram Walker's liquor operations had been taken over by Allied Lyons plc for approximately £1 billion. At that time, Allied Lyons plc became Allied Distillers Ltd. During the distillery's 'silent' period Don Raitt stayed on as operations manager and continued to fight for its survival. He was there to celebrate its re-opening, remaining in the post for a further six months.

In January 1990 Allied Distillers Ltd acquired the spirits operation of the brewer Whitbread & Co Ltd, which included Laphroaig distillery, where Iain Henderson had recently been appointed manager. Ian Miller makes the point that "Once we had Laphroaig as well as Ardbeg there was no need for two managers, one could run both distilleries, so after Iain Henderson had been there a while, Don Raitt moved on to Pulteney in Wick. We were extremely fortunate in Iain and his wife, Carol – they provided a very stable period."

By this time, the level of the 'whisky loch' was beginning to fall and the outlook for Scotch whisky was altogether brighter, with export levels on the rise (See Newsletter page 55). Iain Henderson says "Allied had just entered into a joint venture with Suntory to promote the Ballantine's blend in the Far East, and so it was anticipated that greater quantities of malts would be needed for the blend. Accordingly, the decision was taken to reopen Ardbeg. When I arrived, the distillery was in working condition, but was seriously run down, with warehouse roofs falling in."

Master Blender, Robert Hicks was instrumental in getting Ardbeg up and running again. Like Henderson, he noted the dilapidation of parts of the distillery site, saying "The distillery had suffered during the seven years of closure. We put a decent amount of money in to start it up and to renew things. However, major capital expenditure would be needed to bring it back to a pre-shutdown position.

"I flew over to Islay from Glasgow to help with the setting up. Essentially, I had been sent over to 'tune' the still. The Ballantine's blend was quite sweet and fruity, and although Ardbeg was a lovely whisky, it hadn't the sweetness we required for Ballantine's. Over the years, Hiram Walker had developed a method of getting sweet, fruity spirit from all its stills, tuning them to give the high esters, the really sweet notes.

They had been running at about 30 minutes and I brought the cut down to 20 minutes. I think it is down to about 15 minutes now, while Laphroaig runs for about 45 minutes. (See Chapter Five.)

"Until it closed in 1981, Ardbeg had been running consistently at 80-90ppm on the malting floors, although the malt could go to 100-110ppm because it's just coating. When the distillery re-opened in 1989 Allied took the decision not to peat so heavily so that the spirit was more usable in blends. 45ppm was the aim and Port Ellen Maltings was employed to supply malt, although it was initially just at 30-35ppm."

Laphroaig and Ardbeg manager Iain Henderson had first worked on Islay at Bunnahbahain distillery, where he was employed as the engineer. He then spent 14 years at Glenlivet on Speyside before returning to Islay to manage Laphroaig. "Some of the old staff who had previously worked at Ardbeg were re-recruited," he recalls, "and when the place was running we had six operators. When it reopened, that meant for a while every distillery on the island was working, except, of course, for Port Ellen. When I went there Ardbeg had 22,000 casks in the warehouses. Quite a lot of stock! It was all for the Ballantine's blend, though Hiram Walker had bottled some as a ten-year-old. However, Allied had no intention of selling any as a single malt.

"I put in a lot of hours at Ardbeg. The spirit was very inconsistent when distilling started, and to improve the consistency one thing we did was to take more care in the milling process. At that time the purifier on the spirit still wasn't working, it was blocked off because it had cracked. The distillery was run pretty quickly because what Allied wanted was bulk. Part of the inconsistency was also due to inaccurate low wines to feints ratios. There isn't an automatic balance at Ardbeg, and one of the problems was that all the low wines and all the feints had been pumped into each charge. We eventually got it balanced and running well.

"In 1990 we made half a million litres of spirit, because of the potential growth in sales of Ballantine's, and because it's not economic to run a distillery like Ardbeg on a small scale. It makes sense to run it full out or not at all. We worked a five-day week, but had longer silent seasons than at Laphroaig, maybe lasting 12 weeks."

However, ownership of Laphroaig and Ardbeg presented difficulties for Allied Distillers Ltd, as Ian Miller explains. "Ardbeg became a problem for us because Laphroaig was selling well as a single malt. We would have had a problem trying to market two heavily-peated Islays." Robert Hicks comments that "Someone once said 'You never want to own an Islay distillery,' and Allied ended up with two! By 1992 we were selling quite a bit of malt, not a lot, but about 20,000 to 25,000 cases per year.

"Allied decided to employ a Malts Manager and Jeremy Wetherhead was appointed to the position. In 1994 he projected that by 2010 he would have Laphroaig selling 90,000 cases a year, which was four times what we were selling then. We actually passed that target in about 1997/8. Jeremy wanted to sell Ardbeg too, but he did not appear to get the support, so only a very limited amount was bottled. We decided to keep Ardbeg running, and while we didn't actually put it up for sale, we let it be known we were open to offers. It was a case of keeping it running or it would fall to bits."

Between 1991 and 1995 Ardbeg was operating at around one-third of its capacity, but in July 1996 Allied Distillers closed the distillery down once again. Iain Henderson notes that "Towards the end, we managed to extend the life of the distillery by about six months when the wash charger cracked and we had to bypass it.

"I'd always prefer to run distilleries rather than shut them down, and when it came to closure there was the chance for any of the guys who wanted it to move to Laphroaig, but nobody did. The six operators all took the redundancy package and the place became nothing but a warehouse. The Laphroaig warehousing squad worked it. We emptied some of the warehouses with bad roofs, put the casks into the better warehouses, and a lot was taken to Allied's Dumbarton site. Some of the warehouse roofs were repaired while the distillery was closed.

"There was a feeling that it would be good for Laphroaig if the whole Islay category was doing well"

"The official line was that it was closing because the company had two distilleries side by side and they would never market them both as single malts. Ardbeg was surplus to Allied's requirements. I had to show around people who were interested in buying it. Suntory wanted it, the Hillman family who owned Burn Stewart Distillers at one time wanted it, Chivas looked at it, Glenmorangie was interested, and so was Mark Reynier."

Mark Reynier was an experienced wine and spirits merchant and founder of the London-based independent bottlers Murray McDavid Ltd. In 1993 he had commissioned Allied

Distillers to fill 100 casks of Ardbeg, and as he recalls, "When we asked if they would distil another batch for us, they said no, so we asked if we could buy the distillery. They said no to that, too!

"I came up to Islay with my business partner Simon Coughlin in February 1996 to look at Ardbeg, and I was bewitched, not so much by the whisky as by the setting. I'd pestered Allied to sell Ardbeg to us for several years, and even gone to their offices in Bristol, where I was told that they were prepared to sell the distillery now, and I was welcome to bid for it. At a second meeting I was asked to put a bid on the table. I'd been professionally advised that £4 million was the right figure, given the level of stock and just how bad a state the place was in."

Iain Miller's view of the sale of Ardbeg is that "Allied was very responsible and didn't want to sell the distillery to just anyone. There was a feeling that it would be good for Laphroaig if the whole Islay category was doing well, and if Ardbeg was being successfully marketed by someone. Allied was not committed to selling to the highest bidder. Glenmorangie was seen to have done a good job promoting its single malt, and it was thought they would invest in Ardbeg and do a good job there too. "

Iian Henderson comments that "I couldn't understand the philosophy of selling the distillery to a competitor who was going to spend money on it and create a rival to Laphroaig." Nonetheless, in February 1997 Glenmorangie plc acquired Ardbeg distillery and stocks for a price of £7 million, of which £5.5 million was the valuation of maturing spirit. Another, happier, chapter in the chequered history of Ardbeg was about to unfold.

How We Began

In spite of Scotch whisky's ancient origins, it is only in the past few decades that it has featured prominently as an international item of trade. Although it has been the world's most travelled whisky since British Colonial times, Scotch began the rise to its present pre-eminence in world markets following the ending of prohibition in the United States in 1933.

But even before that, in 1930, a major Canadian distilling company, Hiram Walker-Gooderham and Worts Limited, was far-sighted enough to seek a stake in what was to become the world's most sought-after whisky.

To ensure a guaranteed share of supplies of the best Scotch whisky available, it acquired an interest in three Scotch whisky companies. This was the basis of the formation of Hiram

The waters of Loch Lomond, famed in legend and song, are used in Hiram Walker's Scotch whisky blends promoted worldwide.

Walker and Sons (Scotland) Limited, as well as the decision to build at Dumbarton the then largest grain distillery in Europe.

The original Hiram Walker, a grain merchant from Massachusetts, had by 1859 built his first grain distillery on a 250-acre site on the Canadian bank of the Detroit River, where the eponymous town of Walkerville now stands. This flourished successfully, becoming a major Canadian enterprise. In 1926 the Hiram Walker business was acquired by Toronto businessman Harry Hatch and his associates, who merged it with another old-established firm of distillers he had acquired only two years previously, Gooderham and Worts.

Since then, the merged organisation has become an international group, the third largest distilling company in the world. And in 1980 Hiram Walker-Gooderham and Worts Limited diversified into the energy field by merging with another Canadian company to form the present holding company for Hiram Walker and Sons (Scotland) Limited called Hiram Walker Resources Limited. Its policy of continuing heavy investment since 1930 in the expansion and development of Hiram Walker and Sons (Scotland) Limited has been of great benefit to the Scotch whisky industry and to Scotland. But another important contribution has been the provision of a highly efficient world-wide marketing organisation which has played no small part in enabling Hiram Walker's brands to be available for discriminating consumers in almost every part of the world.

Since its entry into the Scotch whisky business, the Canadian parent company has shown a high degree of respect for the jealously guarded traditions of Scotch whisky production and this is reflected in the management autonomy of its thoroughly Scottish subsidiary.

6

ARDBEG
FINEST ISLAY SINGLE MALT
SCOTCH WHISKY

Ardbeg Distillery is to be found on the South East coast of Islay. Built close to the waters edge it over-looks the coast of Kintyre, and on a clear day the coast of Ireland some 20 miles South, may be viewed.

Surrounded by heather covered hills supplying an ample quantity of water, the chief characteristic being its softness and purity, it was ideally situated for both the smugglers and the original founders of the Distillery; the former in operation for many years until their practices were discovered and the place destroyed, the founders, who built on the original site and were registered according to the Government requirements in 1815.

Situated at such a far distance from the nearest port, (3½ miles) it very quickly became a thriving community; forty families were housed by the company and a small two teacher school established. (With the movement of time and modern methods of travel, only eleven families remain, the other employees travelling from all parts of the Island). Unlike the other Distilleries on the Island, Ardbeg was not only able to boast a 'pier' but a regular passenger, mail and cargo vessel, twice weekly; not only a valued service to the community, but an added prestige to the Distillery. Ardbeg's distinctive flavour has played a large part in its continued demand, no less so than in its export to the States during the period of prohibition.. Indeed, it was one of the few Distilleries to continue production during the depression years.

Despite installation of new plant, Ardbeg has re-mained faithful to the traditional methods of production of Malt Whisky. Peat plays a major part in the smoking of the malted barley, the flavour of which is predominant in the final product; no less important are the gleaming copper stills, the shape of which have remained unchanged since installation.

Only in the latter years has Ardbeg bottled on its own behalf. Previously the greater part was utilised in the blending of established and well recognised brands of whisky. Despite the great demand on Ardbeg, production has increased at a controlled level, (now standing at 400,000 gals. per Annum) thus maintaining the unique quality that is 'Ardbeg.'

ARDBEG DISTILLERY LIMITED
ISLE OF ISLAY ARGYLL SCOTLAND
ESTABLISHED 1815

Hiram Walkers corporate literature c1977

Barley ready for malting at Ardbeg

Traditional turning and airing at Ardbeg

Gilbert Johnson turning the malt floor at Ardbeg.

Ardbeg distillery from the southwest, c1981. Note that all the warehousing and the big house on the shore still stand, but were subsequently knocked down later that year.

Whisky boom for Islay distil

ALLIED Distillers have topped up their recent announcement of plans to bring two Speyside distilleries out of mothballs with news of another proposed re-opening — of their Ardbeg Distillery in Islay.

The company, part of the Allied-Lyons Group, said yesterday that their triple Scotch of re-openings was...

Company complete Scotch

■ Ardbeg Distillery, Islay . . . Allied Distillers "delig

ALLIED DISTILLERS TO RE-OPEN ARDBEG DISTILLERY

A further indication of the recent upturn in the Scotch Whisky industry was given when Allied Distillers Ltd, part of the Allied-Lyons Group, announced that the Company is to re-open Ardbeg Distillery on the island of Islay.

The announcement comes only a few weeks after Allied Distillers purchased two mothballed malt distilleries from United Distillers with the intention of returning them to full production at an early date. The re-opening of these three distilleries is a result of the continuing steady growth for Allied Distillers' brands.

The re-opening of Ardbeg will create ten jobs on Islay and this will supplement the 25 new jobs created at Imperial and Glentauchers Distilleries, which are located in the Speyside area of Scotland.

The company has said the recruitment would commence immediately with Ardbeg

being operational again before the end of this year.

Ardbeg is a distinctive malt whisky which will be used mainly in blending Ballantine's Scotch whisky.

David Jarvis, Managing Director of Allied Distillers Ltd, said: "We are delighted to re-open Ardbeg. This represents a hat-trick of distillery announcements over the past few weeks and is indicative of our belief that good times are ahead and set to continue for the Scotch Whisky industry.

"Allied Distillers is a major player in the industry with our brands Ballantine's, Teacher's, Old Smuggler and Cream of the Barley and the re-opening of these three distilleries is a strategic move in line with our overall plans for the future development of the business. We are pleased that this fine distillery will be back in production very soon."

Various press releases announcing the re-opening of Ardbeg distillery in 1989. Being one of three recently re-opened distilleries, Allied clearly had plans for Ardbeg; that was until they acquired Laphroaig just a few months later!

THE SCOTCH WATCH

ISSUE NUMBER NINE

FOCUS ON SALES SERVICE — CENTRE PAGES

ARDBEG RE-OPENING

Increasing demand for Ballantine's Scotch Whisky around the world has prompted Allied Distillers Ltd (the parent company of George Ballantine & Son Ltd) to re-open the Ardbeg Distillery, which contributes an exceptional malt whisky to the Ballantine's blend.

First established in 1815, Ardbeg ceased distilling in 1981. However, the Manager, Don Raitt and his skeleton crew have kept the distillery in working order and continued supply of all Ardbeg malt whisky which had been stockpiled for use by Ballantine's and other blends.

Ardbeg is situated on the south-east coast of the island of Islay in an isolated area of great natural beauty. The malt produced there has a unique peaty flavour and also benefits from the exceptionally soft and pure waters drawn from nearby lochs Uigidale and Iarnon.

The re-opening of Ardbeg will create new jobs on Islay and is testimony to the recent upturn of the Scotch Whisky industry. It follows the recent re-opening by Allied Distillers of the Imperial and Glentauchers distilleries which are located in the Speyside area of Scotland.

According to Allied Distillers Managing Director, David Jarvis: "We are delighted to re-open Ardbeg and pleased that this fine distillery is back in production. The re-opening is a strategic move in line with our overall plans for the future development of the business and is indicative of our belief that good times are ahead and set to continue for Ballantine's and the Scotch Whisky industry."

Cheers! Don Raitt, Manager of Ardbeg, toasts the re-opening of the distillery.

WHEN IN KYOTO...

Resplendent in the Kimono, Ballantine's Chairman David Jarvis and Managing Director Mark Butterworth could only be in Japan. But what were they up to? Find out on Page 11.

Ballantine's
THE SUPERB SCOTCH

THE
GLENMORANGIE
YEARS

CHAPTER THREE

Ladders to the 2nd floor of the maltings (opposite)

"Allied Distillers was pleased Ardbeg had gone into loving hands," says Dr Bill Lumsden, Glenmorangie's head of distilling and whisky creation. "They were incredibly helpful, especially Robert Hicks, but really the whole team. I believe we were actually the second-highest bidder. We believe we got a bargain and that £4m would not have covered the value of the stock, let alone the distillery and the brand equity." Having paid £7.7m, plus many more millions on refurbishing and re-equipping Ardbeg, the distillery has been transformed from 'pauper to prince.'

"I'm sure they would also have seen the condition of the distillery, which was badly in need of some 'TLC,' and that's me being extremely diplomatic"

Bill Lumsden states that "As a company we were always interesting in expanding our portfolio of brands. Ardbeg did come up and it was arguably one of the very few single malt brands that truly had cult status among aficionados. One of my roles when I was working with United Distillers was conducting quality audits at Port Ellen Maltings. The manager there had a nice display of the various Islay bottles and Ardbeg was the one that always intrigued me. It was very hard to get hold of and people spoke about it in hushed whispers. It genuinely was a fantastic whisky, but the fact that you just could not get it gave it the cult status. It was poles apart in terms of style from anything we owned, so it was very interesting to us.

"I'm sure a lot of people would have looked at the distillery and thought that it was a real niche category and I'm sure they would also have seen the condition of the distillery, which was badly in need of some 'TLC,' and that's me

being extremely diplomatic. We saw it as a challenge. It is an ongoing challenge to bring it up to the standard we like, but then I see it as a lifetime challenge to bring all my distilleries up to that standard."

Clearly, the most urgent priority for Ardbeg's new owners was to re-commission the distillery, and to that end, long-serving Glen Moray manager Ed Dodson was despatched to Islay, where he spent six months getting Ardbeg up and running once again. "They chose me to go and start the distillery up again because I was the only person who had worked in a distillery with old equipment like Ardbeg had," says Ed. "I'd been in the industry since 1963, and the equipment mostly dated from the 1950s or '60s, or even earlier. No one had spent much money on the place!"

Ed was one of the three people from Glenmorangie who went over to examine the distillery before the company bought it. His first impressions were that it was very run down and needed a lot of money spending on it. "Maybe Allied would have liked to knock it down," he muses, "but that would have been expensive, and not good for their image, I suppose! I don't like seeing any distillery closed, and it was great to be there to see Ardbeg reopen and to be a part of it.

"When I went there I was working 15 or 16 hours a day, six days a week. It was the only way to get the job done. We had to replace the old cast iron hot liquor tank in the mash house, and the steam pipes, and there were lots of 'health and safety' issues to address. With us buying the distillery and getting it going again, we obviously had to comply with all the legislation. The mash tun really needed replacing, as it was cast iron and too low in the ground, so it was difficult to work with. But that wasn't replaced till after I'd left."

The head of the low wines and spirit still was riveted and dated from before the Second World War. It had to be replaced later, but at the time of the distillery start-up it was in good enough condition to use. The boiler had been installed back in 1965 and although Ed and his team did not have too much faith in it, they managed to make it work reliably. One washback was missing, and had to be replaced, along with two that were in particularly bad condition. The replacement washbacks came from the silent Hillside distillery near Montrose, but they were too large for use at Ardbeg, and had to be cut down to fit.

"There were two guys still employed at Ardbeg," notes Ed Dodson, "Wardie and Ruari Macintyre, and I initially took on two who had previously worked there. One was Alex Livingstone, and the other was The Gow, both of whom are still there. We mashed for the first time on 16 June 1997, and when we started to produce, I didn't expect the first spirit to be any good because the washbacks were sour. They'd had water standing in them, and it was very peaty water at that. But it was actually pretty good, and once we really got it running it was very good. I was surprised by just how fruity it was and how that helps to mask the smoky tar notes from the heavily peated malt. We got the first spirit at 2am on 20 June." The distillery ran until the first week in August then closed down for the 'silent season,' as was usual on Islay. That provided the opportunity to do some more work on the plant, though Ed Dodson recalls the difficulty of obtaining the services of specialist tradesmen on the island, and many were brought from the mainland, which took time as well as costing money.

Bill Lumsden says "We operated it in 1997 just to tuck some stock under our belts, but then we had to close down to start the first phase of repairs as the distillery simply would not have gone on. We replaced some copper work, pipe work and electrics which just weren't working. At this time I was Glenmorangie distillery manager. We went over and threw our tuppence worth in. On this visit I was intrigued by a shoe box stuck to the wall which I thought was some kind of local good luck symbol. Eventually I asked one of the guys about it and he went over and pulled it off, revealing an exposed electrical junction box! It is that sort of thing we saw about the plant, so to say it was held together with chewing gum, Sellotape and string was not too far removed from the truth.

"The Islay people were so friendly, and everyone was dead keen to see the place up and running again"

Duncan Logan had previously served as Ardbeg brewer for 35 years, and he was a great asset as he knew so much about the running of the distillery and its equipment, helping out when there were problems or queries. Ed Dodson notes that "The Islay people were so friendly, and everyone was dead keen to see the place up and running again. Co-operation with the locals generally was fantastic. I enjoyed my six months there, though I didn't have much of a social life as I was working so hard. I stayed in a chalet at the Machrie Hotel, and if you were in the hotel to eat or for a drink, and guests found out you were a distillery manager, you'd never get to bed. You'd be up drinking till 2am, and that just wasn't really on. Overall, it was quite an honour to be asked to go over and do what I did, and I'm proud to have played my part in it all."

Ed Dodson's assistant manager at Glen Moray was Stuart Thomson, and with Ardbeg in production once again and Ed heading back east, the decision was taken to send Stuart on a six months secondment to run the recently-acquired distillery.

As Stuart recalls, "When I first visited Islay it was to see Ardbeg, prior to a six months spell there. I went to Ardbeg on the understanding I could go back to my job in Elgin at the end of the six months if I didn't like it. Being a whisky person it was fantastic driving from Port Ellen, passing Laphroaig and Lagavulin - such great Scotch whisky names. When I got to Ardbeg I stopped my car at the top of the road and let my collie dog out for a call of nature. I looked down on the distillery and even from that distance I couldn't believe the state of the place. The dog took one look at the distillery and instead of getting back in the car he headed off in the opposite direction! I couldn't really blame him. I wondered just what I'd let myself in for.

> *"We found quite a lot of empty casks, which had just leaked their contents over time, as they'd never been checked for years"*

"I'd not been married long and my wife Jackie was pregnant, so I had gone over by myself and stayed for three days. The distillery was a mess, but Islay has this mystique about it, and after three days I'd already been hooked. I went home and told Jackie Ardbeg was 'lovely.' A little lie. When she actually saw it for the first time she looked at me and said "You lying ******!

"The warehousing was in a horrific state. Number 3 had a big hole in the roof, despite having stock in it. We had to move it all out to other places before we could start repair work. We found quite a lot of empty casks, which had just leaked their contents over time, as they'd never been checked for years."

During Stuart's tenure as manager the distillery plant was progressively upgraded, with the installation of a new mash tun and a replacement spirit still. Bill Lumsden notes that "During the second major shut down we replaced the mashtun. The marketing department wanted to keep the old-fashioned 'rakes and plough' mashtun. However, as someone who had worked with one of these older style mashtuns at my first distillery and as a scientist on the technology of mashing I was equally adamant that we should not keep it. So we reached a compromise where I replaced the guts of the mashtun with semi-lauter steering gear and kept the old cast iron plates which were fitted over the new stainless steel shell."

Inevitably, expenditure is ongoing at any distillery, and as Stuart notes, "Apart from anything else, you have to paint the outside two or three times a year because moisture works its way out of the stone. That costs around £20,000 a year alone. People who had lived in Ardbeg all their lives never expected it to come back to life, and what we did as a company by reviving it stood us in good stead locally."

A range of new and attractively packaged Ardbeg single malt bottlings was gradually developed in order to boost sales and enhance the brand image (see Chapter Six), while a great deal of attention was also focused on creating an attractive and welcoming visitor centre. Accordingly, one of the disused malt kilns was converted into the Old Kiln Café, which opened in 1998, providing a rare opportunity for visitors to obtain refreshments while visiting an Islay distillery. Before long, the Ardbeg café was one of the favourite eating places on the island for both visitors and locals alike. The kiln conversion also housed the distillery shop, acting as a showcase for Ardbeg bottlings, along with branded clothing and gift items.

The café and shop is the domain of Jackie Thomson, whose initial impressions of Islay were coloured by an event taking place far from the Hebrides, and one that has become highly significant in modern history. "I first came to Ardbeg the day that Princess Diana died," she says. "August 1997. Stuart was already there and he drove me all over, showing me Islay. It seemed to take so long to get anywhere – I thought it was a much smaller island than it turned out to be.

"There was a phone booth in the corner of the old mash house, so I phoned my mum to tell her all about the place, and she was very quiet. She told me about Diana and the car crash in Paris. That unfortunate event will always be etched in my mind with the day I arrived on Islay. I had to finish my season working in the Glenmorangie distillery visitor centre, before I could join Stuart at Ardbeg to take on the role of visitor centre manager. Stuart had been assistant manager under Ed Dodson at Glen Moray distillery from 1993 and also worked at Glenmorangie for 12 years before that, where his father was assistant manager. I started work at Glenmorangie visitor centre and we put together the new one in 1997/98. We got married while we were at Glenmorangie."

The Old Kiln Café has been a tremendous success, bringing additional focus to this part of the island and in a small way, helping to restore a sense of community. Having spent over 10 years on Islay, Jackie is wholeheartedly committed to her role there and is sanguine about island life, summing it up as "On Islay your life is played out with a microphone. It could just be a quiet song, but instead it's a disco! I don't mean that in a bad way – it's just the way it is on an island."

In 2004 Ardbeg experienced yet another change of ownership, when the Macdonald family, owners of Glenmorangie plc, sold the company, including Ardbeg, Glenmorangie and Glen Moray distilleries, to the LVMH Group for £300 million. LVMH (Louis Vuitton Moet Hennessy) has its headquarters in Paris and specialises in luxury brands, including Moet and Chandon, Krug and Dom Perignon champagnes, Hennessy Cognac and wines from a number of New World vineyards.

To the dismay of many Ardbeg fans, August 2006 saw Stuart Thomson announce his intention of resigning from his post as distillery manager at Ardbeg

The purchase of Glenmorangie by LVMH was followed by the release of the two most exclusive and expensive Ardbeg presentations of all time, and while in keeping with the ethos of LVMH, Ardbeg's global brand director Hamish Torrie is keen to point out that "The 1965 bottling and the Double Barrel releases (see Chapter Six) were definitely not influenced by LVMH's purchase of Glenmorangie. Both ideas had been on the slate long before LVMH came along. They have no input into the distilleries and the whisky selection. As far as Ardbeg's concerned they just say 'keep going as you are.'"

To the dismay of many Ardbeg fans, August 2006 saw Stuart Thomson announce his intention of resigning from his post as distillery manager at Ardbeg, subsequently moving back to the mainland to pursue other projects. Jackie Thomson continued in her role as visitor centre manager, while Jura distillery manager and *Ileach* Mickey Heads was recruited to take Stuart's place. Mashman and stillman Ruaraidh Macintyre ('Mackie') says "We were all apprehensive about getting a new manager, but it's great that Mickey is a local. He's got the best interests of Ardbeg and the island in mind."

"I was cock-a-hoop about getting Mickey Heads as the new manager"

Bill Lumsden goes so far as to say "I was cock-a-hoop about getting Mickey Heads as the new manager. You know all the managers and the ones you hope will apply for the post and Mickey was absolutely at the top of my list. It was a wrench for him to leave the Isle of Jura but we thought he would be perfect for the position and he has already done a fantastic job there. The distillery is as buzzing as I can ever remember it. He has a really long period of experience and history, so any of the little production problems just don't faze him. He has taken the distillery by the scruff of the neck and re-invigorated it."

"The whisky's good – so you don't need to change the place," declares Mickey Heads. "I'm really just carrying it all forward. I see myself as just a caretaker. Somebody will always come along after you, and maybe do it differently. So you just do it as well as you can, and with as much passion as you can."

Stillman and mashman Alistair Johnston ('Asha') says "Stuart and Jackie put Ardbeg back on the map. Their contribution has been massive. Jackie's one of the hardest workers I've ever seen. She's got so much passion and enthusiasm."

Mashman Archie McKechnie ('Yogi') notes that "The place looks so much better now than it did when I came here. You wouldn't have wanted to be working here when Allied had it," and stillman and mashman Malcolm Livingstone ('Azza') echoes that point. "The place is beyond recognition now compared to what it was like before it reopened," he declares. "Doors were hanging off and everything was dirty and untidy, with weeds everywhere. Now it's all white and clean and tidy."

No.1 maltings and kiln being refurbished in 1997

No.1 maltings and kiln, now converted into the Old Kiln Café, visitor centre and office

Jackie Thomson

Ardbeg distillery from the east

THE WHISKY
MAKERS

CHAPTER FOUR

One of the key tools in selling Scotch whisky to the world is the image of a lovingly hand-crafted product, made in remote parts of the highlands and islands, using traditional ingredients and methods handed down from generation to generation of dedicated and skilful local men. Yet walk into some malt distilleries today and you are confronted by an array of computer consoles, with just one man per shift controlling the entire production process with the aid of a mouse – and not the kind that nibbles away at the malt, either. But not all distilleries are like that. In some cases, what the marketing personnel tell consumers about personal input is entirely true. And nowhere is this more evident than at Ardbeg.

Certainly there is a degree of useful automation, and the raw material of malt is no longer made on site, but walk into the stillhouse and there is not a computer console in sight. At quiet times the duty stillman may be found sitting in an ancient, wooden, kitchen chair, perusing a copy of *Boat Fishing*. This magazine is a favourite read in a distillery where most of the operators either own fishing boats, were previously fishermen, or served at sea in the Royal or Merchant Navy in the great tradition of island-dwellers the world over. Even distillery manager Mickey Heads has just purchased his first boat.

Unlike many distilleries today, a large proportion of the spirit produced at Ardbeg is filled into casks and matured on site. There are no 'flying warehouse squads' here, moving from distillery to distillery, filling casks destined for maturation in large warehouse complexes far from the spirit's place of creation. At Ardbeg a dedicated warehouse team which knows the nuances and niceties of maturation can point out the choicest casks maturing in the finest locations.

Of course, in these days when few people live all their lives in the place where they were born, not everyone who works at Ardbeg is an *Ileach*, as native islanders are known in Gaelic. But, as is so often the case, incomers enrich the community, and soon come to share the same passion and commitment to Ardbeg as those who are able to trace their roots on the island back through several generations and can boast impressive distilling pedigrees. However, islanders still make up the bulk of the Ardbeg workforce, and as the village of Port Ellen is noted for its prolific use of nicknames, staff members are rarely known by their Christian names, as will become obvious in the following pages!

Ardbeg is in production 24 hours a day, six and a half days per week, and operates three eight hour shifts each day, with two members of production staff on duty at any one time. Most members of the production team are dual-trained to control either the mashing or distilling sides of the operation, and are paired up to work together on a long-term basis, frequently swapping between distilling and mashing week by week.

As Ruaraidh Macintyre ('Mackie') recalls, "I started work in the stillhouse in 1989, you just did the one job at that time. If you were a mashman you were a mashman, and that was it." The warehouse squad usually comprises three or four members, at least two of whom have been trained for mashing and/or distilling duties, and can provide holiday and sickness cover as required. There are currently four warehouses at Ardbeg, and due to the demolition of several in the past there is now an idiosyncratic numbering system, hence the current warehouses are numbered 3, 4, 9 and 10.

Spending any significant length of time in the company of the Ardbeg staff it soon becomes apparent that there is an extremely strong sense of community and mutual respect among them, despite the many jokes and humorous put-downs that characterise any group conversation. As warehouseman Douglas Bowman ('Dugga') says, "You hear people talking about Ardbeg and you know you're part of it all. It's a good feeling. Other guys would leave their distilleries to be part of Ardbeg. We're close and we get on well. We have fun. There's lots of banter between the production staff and us. We say they get paid more than us just for flicking a switch!"

According to Archie McKechnie ('Yogi') "I definitely enjoy the job. Everybody gets on well, and there's a great atmosphere. Everybody jokes and slags each other off – but in a good way. Nothing's taken to heart, and there's always a good answer fired back." 'Mackie' declares "Everyone will say to a man that they enjoy working here. There's lots of talk among the various guys who work in distilleries on the island about who's got the best stillhouse and who makes the best whisky and so on – but it's all a bit of nonsense! At the end of the day, if we had a major problem we could go to Laphroaig or Lagavulin and they'd help out straight away."

Ed Dodson says of his arrival at Ardbeg to re-commission the distillery for new owners Glenmorangie in 1997, "I was very impressed by the guys. They loved Ardbeg and were so pleased it was being revived. They knew they had a good product and took a lot of pride in the place. They were great workers. "

One of those 'guys' was Alexander Woodrow, or 'Wardie,' Until his retirement in 2007, Wardie was the longest-serving member of the Ardbeg team, having worked at the distillery for 47 years. He recalls "I was born in Duich, between Port Ellen

and Bowmore, in a wee tin house at the side of the road 62 years ago. My father was a shepherd at the farm there. He got a job at Ardbeg distillery when I was two and we moved there. He was a maltman. At first I was living in another tin house again! There were five or six of those at the distillery but they were knocked down later. After that, we lived in the Big House, which used to belong to the Hays and had recently been divided up into six flats when we went there.

"The house was right onto the sea, and the waves would crash up against the bedroom windows when the weather was really rough. Sometimes it was just like being at sea. Seaweed would pile up against the still house door in bad weather. There would be about a dozen families living at Ardbeg when I was growing up, and there were ruins of other cottages round about; there was a good wee shop, too.

"I left school at 14 and went to work on Ardbeg Farm, which was a dairy farm. I was there for four years and then the distillery manager, Dougie MacIntyre took me on. My first job was in the malt barns, turning the malt, and I enjoyed that. It was hard work, but good fun. We got two wee drams for helping the warehousemen fill lorries with casks once or twice a week, and the work was always more fun after those! My father liked a dram, and he liked to drink the wash in particular. A lot of the men did in those days."

Until the 1980s, distillery workers received several, semi-official measures of whisky per day, usually of high-strength, 'new-make' spirit straight from the stills, and if a particularly dirty or unpleasant task had to be undertaken, they would be rewarded with a 'dirty dram,' as it was known. Inevitably, this led to some rather intoxicated employees from time to time. 'Wardie' recalls "One day, I had a bottle of whisky in the house, and when we had a break at lunchtime me and this other chap went to the house and we had a few drams. Well, we ended up lying down by the roadside and had a sleep. We were supposed to be back at work at 2pm, but, of course, we weren't. I was suspended for a week that time by Hamish [Scott.] We used to work Christmas and New Year in those days, and I remember one New Year's Day when nobody at work was sober!

"Only myself and Ruaraidh stayed on with Allied when they closed the distillery down. We were sent to work at Laphroaig a lot of the time. When the distillery reopened I was quite surprised to get my job back! When Allied started it up again it was me and Duncan Logan, the brewer, and pretty well the same number of staff as there is now. Lots of buildings had been knocked down after the place closed, including some of the warehouses. I thought it was such a waste. Number 1 was a very good warehouse – that's where the oil tank is now."

Since the retirement of 'Wardie', stillman and mashman James Gillespie has been the most senior Ardbeg operative, though he is universally known as 'The Gow.' "I got my nickname from my father," he explains. "He was 'The Gow' too. He was an accordion player who played tunes composed by Niel Gow. I was born on the island at Bridgend, and worked in farming and the building trade before starting here at Ardbeg in 1989. We were only mashing and distilling half the week then. We distilled Monday to Wednesday and then Thursday and Friday; we put what we had filled into the warehouse. Iain Henderson was running Ardbeg then, as well as Laphroaig. The place was much more run down then than it is now. There was no shop or proper visitor centre.

"There was no production from 1981 to 1989, and when Allied closed it again in July 1996 I was made redundant and I thought that was it, Ardbeg would never open again. But we were lucky, and when Glenmorangie came along and bought the place six months later I was taken back on." 'The Gow's regular shift colleague is Alastair Johnston, or 'Asha,' who says "Every one of my friends has got a nickname, every one. Some are Gaelic. I got mine when I was a boy. There's another guy who works in the maltings at Port Ellen, and he's also Asha. He's known as Big Asha. Well I'm not small, so I don't know just what size he is!

"I'm 51 years old and I was born in Port Ellen. I was a fisherman for 25 years, fishing out of Port Ellen for scallops and lobsters, but I've been here the last five years. A lot of the boys have got boats, although the fishing's got depleted now and there are too many rules and regulations. The boys are doing it as a hobby, just for the pot, because you're not allowed to sell what you catch. Neil and Ruaraidh were also fishing, and we have two boys working here who are ex-Navy. I got to know Stuart and Jackie Thomson and then a job here came along. Stuart and Jackie put Ardbeg back on the map. Their contribution has been massive. Jackie's one of the hardest workers I've ever seen. She's got so much passion and enthusiasm.

"This job is much easier than fishing! I started in the warehouse and then moved into the still house and mash house. I learnt how to do it all from 'The Gow,' and I was doing it by myself sooner than I expected. The first day was a bit nerve-racking, but there's always somebody next door in the mash house if you're not sure." Islay remains a place of distilling dynasties, and 'Asha' explains that "My younger brother, Neil, works here too, and another brother works at Laphroaig. My father was also at Laphroaig, but he's retired now. 'The Gow' across in the mash house is my brother-in-law. That's how it is on Islay!"

Neil Johnston is rather obscurely known as 'Philco,' a nickname which definitely requires explanation. "There was a talent contest in the Ramsay Hall in Port Ellen back in the 1950s," he says, "and my father won it for his singing. He was a pub singer. He was offered the chance to go and record a song for Philco, who made radios at that time, though he never took them up on it. And I got the nickname Philco. There were two boys before me in the family, including 'Asha,' so why I got that nickname I really don't know!

"I'm another ex-fisherman. Most of us here have been at sea – in fact all of us except Drew. Mainly for scallops, prawns, lobsters and crabs. At one time, you'd never leave the fishing to go and work in a distillery. But now distilling is the best job you can get into on Islay. I was eleven years at the fishing, and then I got married. With a wife and a child on the way, the idea of a salary and a steady job became attractive. I loved fishing, but by the time I was doing it there wasn't the same sort of money to be made as when my brother, 'Asha,' was doing it.

"So I came up to Ardbeg to see Ed Dodson who was the manager when it first started up again, and he said the jobs would be advertised. I got an interview, and I was the only one without distillery experience who was taken on. I started in May 1997 and was sent to Laphroaig for three weeks to learn the rudiments of distilling. When Allied had Ardbeg it was always second fiddle to Laphroaig, so when Glenmorangie got the place it was the first time it had really had its own identity for years and years.

"When we started up I was put on with Ruaraidh, who knew what he was doing, and I've been here ever since with him. I've tried to get another partner, but I can't seem to get away from him!" Ruaraidh Macintyre, or 'Mackie' as he is usually known, says "My mother was English but my father was local. His grandfather worked in the same room where I work now. Then it was the dryer room, with a big drum filled with steam, drying the draff for farmers to use as cattle feed. He worked on the job for 20 years.

"I've always lived in Port Ellen, and I was fishing from when I left school. When the distillery was due to reopen in 1989 I applied for a job and got it. At the time I was fishing I remember the old shop and post office at Ardbeg was still working. It was owned by the Cunningham family. When I was about ten years old I used to help a guy who was fishing for lobsters. He'd anchor at the pier at Ardbeg and I'd run up to the shop for crisps and sweets. When the shop closed it was a huge loss. The place was a proper village, but lots of the houses were knocked down.

"Ardbeg as a community pretty much died when they closed the place for ten years. At one time the distillery employed more than 30 people, many in the old malt barns. There were eight to ten on the production side. Once Ardbeg closed people went to other distilleries to work or left altogether."

Another member of the production team with a fine, Islay distilling pedigree is Archie McKechnie, known as 'Yogi.' "I got my nickname because I had a jacket with a furry hood when I was at school, and a boy said one day that I looked like Yogi Bear!" he recalls. "I was born in Bowmore, and my father worked in the warehouses at Laphroaig for many years, after being in the Navy. My great-grandfather was manager at Caol Ila. His name was Gordon, and I didn't known about the Caol Ila connection until it was pointed out to me when Caol Ila produced a book about the place and its history.

"Mt first job was as a labourer on the old Manpower Services scheme, then I went to Machrie golf course where I trained as a green keeper, doing college courses and so forth. After a while I went back to labouring again, and was working on the buildings at Ardbeg with Woodrow when a job came up in the warehouses. I applied and I got it. I started work at Ardbeg in February 1998, and there were three of us in the warehouses at that time. I also learnt the mashing so that I could cover that when necessary, and then in 2005 I got the chance to work full time in the mash house. I got the job when Malcolm Rennie left to become manager at Kilchoman. I just do the mashing, I don't do distilling as well, like some of the boys."

Although no longer on the Ardbeg payroll, Malcolm Rennie is keen to discuss his time at the distillery, noting that "Getting a job at Ardbeg in May 1997 was a great thing for me as I'd been made redundant from Bruichladdich in 1994 when it closed. I was unemployed for a while, and was just doing bits and pieces after that. So it was a great chance to get back into distilling. When I was ten years old my father, John, came over to Islay as a cooper at Bunnahabhain. That was 1980. He ended up as head warehouseman there, and is now retired. I worked in the warehouses at Bunnahabhain for six months after I left school, then joined the Merchant Navy for two and a half years, before going to Bruichladdich to work.

"I remember while Ardbeg was closed I'd go up to see Don Raitt sometimes as I was into motorbikes. He was the caretaker manager, in effect. There was scaffolding on the pagodas at the time. Don had old Nortons and he did repairs on bikes for people. He had his bikes in the old tin shed, the peat shed that was in what is now the car park area. There was a lot of old peat lying around, and we put it into number 3 and number 9 warehouses. We cleared the casks out, put the peat in, then put the casks back. It was really just the 'caff,' the dry bits of peat. The distillery was in a pretty bad state at that time. They had replaced the heating tanks when I started work there in 1997 – that was about all Allied had done.

"The re-opening of Ardbeg was exciting for me. I was there when the first spirit came through. Ed Dodson played a big part in the first six months. When I got the job at Ardbeg I told Stuart [Thomson] I wanted to be more than just stillman/mashman, and Stuart started getting me on management courses. I ended up going over to Glen Moray in March 2003 and was there for six months as assistant manager. I learnt a lot from Ed. It was really due to Stuart that I got the Glen Moray job, he got me into management. All the guys at Ardbeg owe Stuart a lot. It was a great team there. A good bunch of guys. I was sad to leave, but it was onwards and upwards. At Kilchoman now we're making a spirit as heavily peated as Ardbeg."

The departure of Malcolm Rennie to Kilchoman allowed Alec Livingstone ('Azza') the opportunity to move from working with the warehouse squad into a shift job, undertaking mashing and distilling duties. Regarding his nickname, Azza says "I got my nickname because at one time I worked for a plumber and he said I had a habit of going "…Azza was saying!" I was born and bred in Port Ellen, and my father worked at Lagavulin and then was a warehouseman at Port Ellen distillery. Of course, Port Ellen whisky is very sought after now, since the distillery closed in 1983.

"I was at Laphroaig in the early 1970s, working the draff dryer, then I spent nine years in the Royal Navy, getting paid to see the world! When I was back home I was drinking in the White Hart in

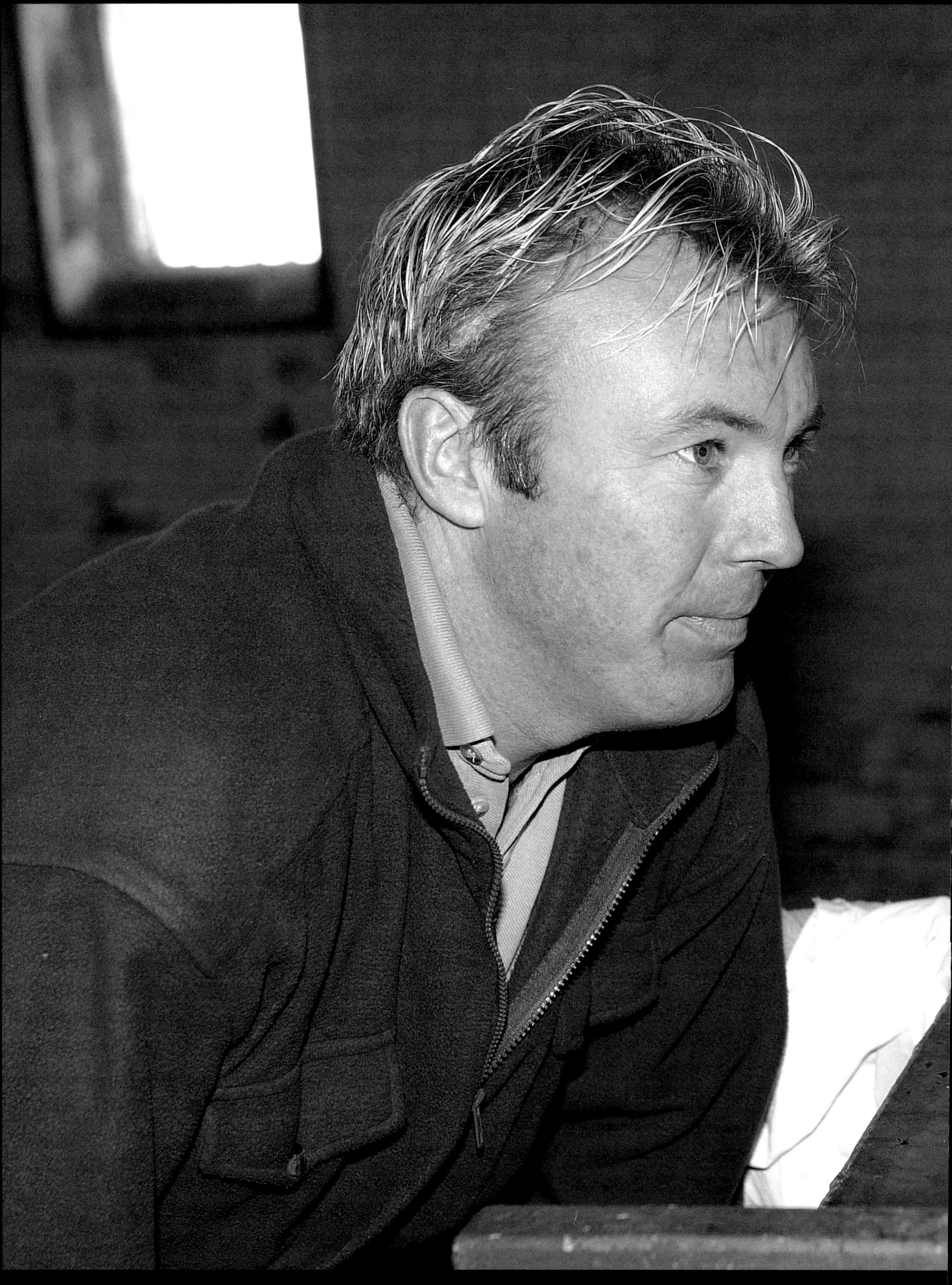

Port Ellen one night and there were some Devon fishermen in the bar. They were fishing for crab and lobster and were looking for a crew member. So I did that for a couple of years, but although it was good money there was no security. I came back to Islay around 1986 and worked for the Manpower Services people, rebuilding walls and working on the visitor centre over at Loch Finlaggan.

"There were rumours that Ardbeg was maybe reopening. The manager at that time, Don Raitt, was an ex-Royal Naval Reserve man, and he knew I'd done all the fire-fighting courses and so forth. I got the job, in 1989, and started by emptying and tidying all the warehouses. I even cleaned the pair of stills with rags and white sand. I was one of five or six guys doing that for a few weeks, and it was hard work. This was before the distillery started up again, of course, but when it did, I began to do the mashing. The place is beyond recognition now compared to what it was like before it reopened. Doors were hanging off and everything was dirty and untidy, with weeds everywhere. Now it's all white and clean and tidy."

Another beneficiary of Malcolm Rennie's move to Kilchoman was Andrew Mullen ('Drew'), the only English member of the Ardbeg team. Born and brought up in north-east England Drew says "I started on a government-funded scheme for nine months, replacing a guy who had moved across to work at Glenmorangie's Glen Moray distillery near Elgin. But then he changed his mind about being there and moved back. After that, I was here temporarily for nine weeks, and then Azza got the mashman/stillman job when Malcolm Rennie left to run Kilchoman, so they needed a replacement warehouseman, and I was taken on for that. My girlfriend had moved here from Durham in 1999, and I loved Scotland and I loved whisky. I visited her for two years and

then moved up. Girl, whisky, Scotland – fantastic!"

Drew's colleague in the warehouse squad is Douglas Bowman, or 'Dugga.' "I was ten years in the Navy before I came here in 1997," he says. "I got into the distillery by chance. I met Ed Dodson at Sports Day in Port Ellen just as they were starting up again. I put my 'CV' in and got the job. My gran and grandpa were both at Laphroaig, as was my great-uncle Ian. I also had an uncle worked at Lagavulin, so there's been a long distilling connection. It's really 'dead men's shoes' to get into it, so I was very lucky to get a start. When I go into the warehouses I know I've had a major hand in building those stows. And I love the smell!"

The newest recruit to the Ardbeg team is Alistair Blair, who works most of the time with the warehouse squad, and who must boast one of the most unusual backgrounds of any distillery worker in Scotland. "For 20 years I taught in a university in Glasgow," he says. "I taught the technical side of how to manufacture artificial limbs to undergraduates and postgraduates. Then I worked at the State Hospital at Carstairs in Lanarkshire [a high-security psychiatric hospital], on the security side of things.

"This is my first job in a distillery. I came to the island three years ago, working as a haulage driver. My wife is an *Ileach*. We decided to come over and settle and have a family. I tried to get a distillery job but there were none going, so I took the transport job. For me it was like an emigration, coming to the island. My ultimate goal was to get into the distillery environment. I joined Ardbeg in July 2007 and it's absolutely fantastic. It's a small, tight-knit workforce, all brilliant guys. I'm very much the new guy, but there's absolutely no hostility. They've taught me so much. My principal job is in the warehouse, but I also double on shift at mashing and distilling for holidays and illness. It's been very much on the job training.

"I found it very easy to fit in on the island. Every day I went to work when I was driving was like a holiday. Everything seemed spectacular. We've got a child now, and he'll be brought up on the island. "I've known Mickey [Heads] since his time at Jura distillery. He stuck out for his professionalism and for being such a knowledgeable and nice guy, so the fact he was manager here was a real pull for me when the job was advertised. He has the reputation of being the doyen of distillery managers."

That 'doyen' of managers may only have been appointed to his present position in 2007, but as an *Ileach*, his knowledge of Ardbeg and the island's other distilleries went back much further."I was born in Port Ellen, but as boys we used to come up to Willie's shop at Ardbeg to buy our sweeties," he remembers. "We'd cycle up on our bikes. It was the only shop at this end of the island. Grandfather was head maltman at Port Ellen distillery, and father was at sea, then he worked in Port Ellen as a stillman. There would be 20-odd people working there at the time. I'd go in to Port Ellen and stack peat when I was a boy, and grandfather even made me a little shiel - the wooden shovels used by maltmen! It was a great place for a boy, but I didn't want to work in a distillery – I either wanted to be a policeman or go to sea.

"After school I worked at Bridgend timber mill and at the peat cutting. Then the assistant brewer at Laphroaig said they were looking for someone, and I started work there on 1st October 1979. I doubled my money. £50.50 was my first Laphroaig wage! I cut peat, cleaned out the lade, which carries water to the distillery, and was part of the squad doing all those sort of jobs, including painting and maintaining the grounds. I did that with 'Asha's father, and I did it for three or four years. There was a lot of peat cutting each spring, and I also did malting and warehousing work. Then I worked with the engineers and I took a shift job when it came up. I was given two weeks' training on the stills and then I was left to it. I was also trained in mashing, and eventually I got the assistant brewer's job.

"In the early 1990s I was assistant brewer on shift, under Iain Henderson. When Alan McConnachie left – he's now managing Benriach on Speyside – I trained in the mash house and then was asked to be brewer. We were running both Laphroaig and Ardbeg at the time. Iain Henderson referred to Ardbeg as a 'sleeping giant.' He had a soft spot for the place, and he knew it made good quality spirit.

"Not that many manager's jobs come along, and so when Jura came up in 1999 I went for it. I threw my hat into the ring and I got it. I loved Jura, and when the Ardbeg manager's vacancy arose I took a lot of weeks mulling it over before I put my 'CV' in. But I like Ardbeg, the distillery and the place, and it was good to come back 'home,' as it were, to get back to Islay. Although Port Ellen is just three miles away you feel totally separate from it at Ardbeg. Totally isolated. My house is in the perfect setting, with views to die for. You don't even hear the distillery. I make a point of enjoying my free time more than I used to. At Jura the distillery was at the bottom of my garden and it was too handy to just keep going in. And it wasn't as if I wanted to get away.

"My father used to go fishing with the guys from Port Ellen distillery. As a boy I played football and golf, and on Jura I did some loch fishing and clay pigeon shooting. When I came back to Islay, to Ardbeg, I decided to get a boat and go line fishing.

The boys have been great at helping me – five of them have got boats of their own. The whisky's good – so you don't need to change the place. I'm really just carrying it all forward. I see myself as just a caretaker. Somebody will always come along after you, and maybe do it differently. So you just do it as well as you can, and with as much passion as you can."

THE WHISKY-MAKERS ON ISLAY

Philco – Neil Johnston

All the distilleries are working far harder now than they were ten years ago. You used to get tourists on Islay, but mainly 'ex-pats,' back to see family at Glasgow Fair holidays and the like. There were never any foreign visitors, but there are lots now with the interest in the whisky. However, the school numbers are way down. Port Ellen primary school has 84 pupils now. There were 180 to 200 when I was there. There are lots of holiday homes on the island, for one thing, and families were a lot bigger. You'd maybe have six to 10 kids, whereas now a big family is three kids.

The Gow – James Gillespie

Islay has changed in that there are fewer residents here now than 30 years ago. Young people have to leave to get jobs. One of my sons and one daughter live and work in London. A few of the young people come back after a while, but not many. However, the whisky industry on Islay is going pretty well at present. There's more money spent promoting Islay whiskies these days, and the tourist season is getting longer all the time, which is good for local businesses.

Mackie - Ruaraidh Macintyre

Islay goes up and down. When I left school there were loads of jobs. If you wanted a job in a distillery you went and 'put your name in' and you got a job. Wages were very poor then. You only went into distilling if you couldn't get anything else. So I went into the fishing where there was far more money. It's all gone full circle now – a distillery job is very desirable. There are lots of 'white settlers' and house prices have gone up, but lots of people have left the island, so they are replacing them in effect. The children get their degrees on the mainland and will only come back for holidays.

Azza – Alec Livingstone

The number of cars on the island now is crazy. Lots of incomers appear, looking for houses and for jobs. Retired people from the south of England, too, and they want to make the place like where they came from. They all open craft shops! And there are a lot of holiday homes on the island now. A lot of characters on the island have gone. When I started at Laphroaig there were only dungarees. We wore tartan shirts and flat caps to work.

Asha – Alistair Johnston

There have been big changes on Islay in the last 20 years or so. There's ever more tourism, and foreign 'whisky tourists' are a massive thing now. Cheap flights from Scandinavia bring people in. They enjoy their malts, and they are very expensive over there.

Mickey Heads

Islay's as buoyant now as I've ever seen it. All the distilleries have turned up the screw – most are working at full capacity, or close to it.

The workforce in 2007 with new Manager Mickey Heads

Yogi

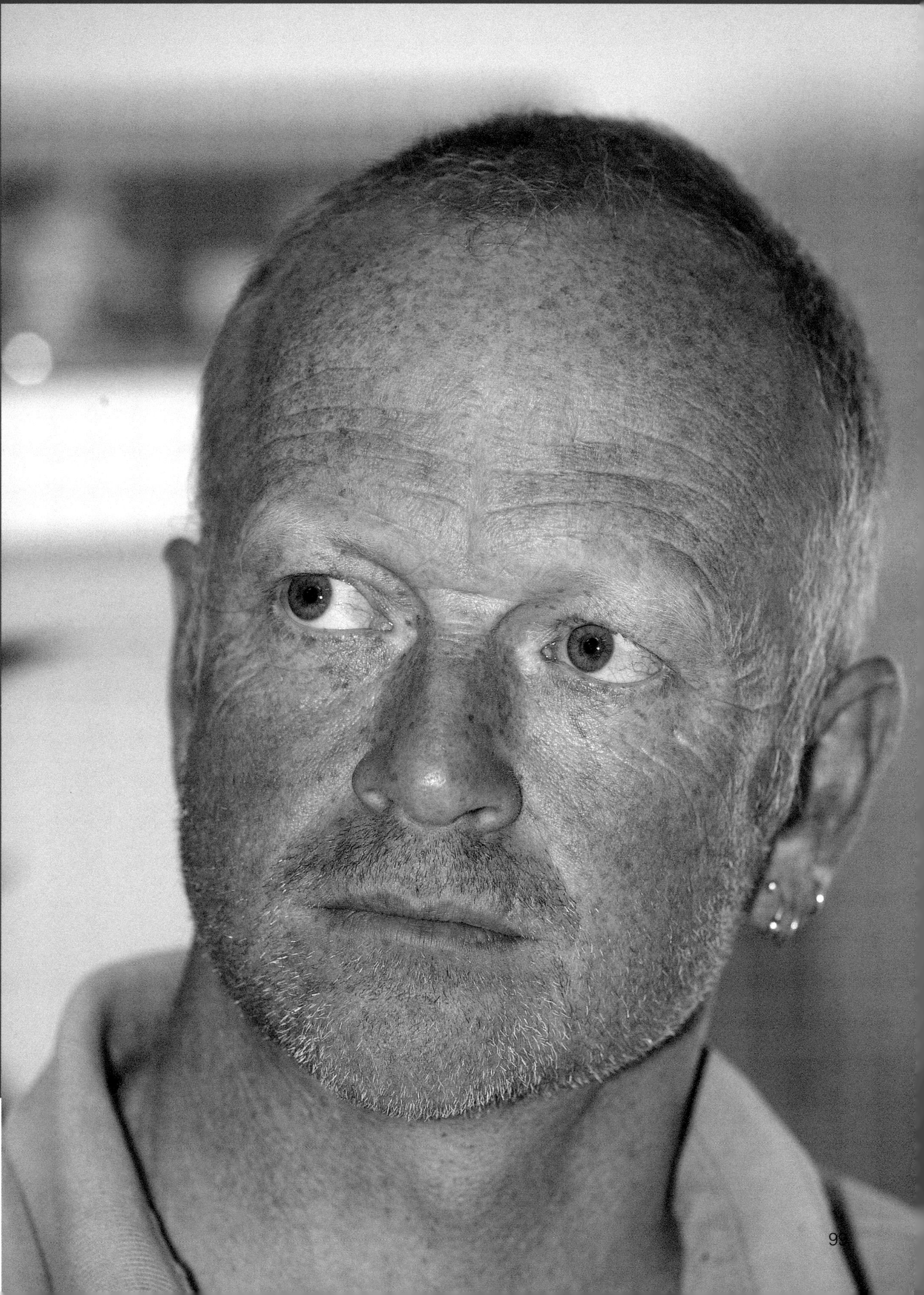

Mickey

MAKING
THE SPIRIT

CHAPTER FIVE

Having met the whisky-makers of Ardbeg it is now time to find out how exactly they go about creating its unique spirit. Although malt whisky is made from a small number of ingredients, using equipment that is really very similar in every distillery, there is a surprisingly vast stylistic spectrum in the whisky we ultimately drink.

Variables that influence the spirit's final style include the water source, level of peating introduced during malting of the barley, the duration of the fermentation process, and the shape and style of stills and the manner in which they are run. Once 'new make' spirit flows from the stills it is then subjected to the many and varied influences of maturation in oak casks. A plentiful supply of pure water is essential for whisky-making, and Ardbeg's 'process' water flows some three miles from Loch Uigeadail via the small hill loch of Airigh nam Beist to Charlie's Dam at the distillery. The water absorbs minerals and particles of peat during its travels, and this is believed to contribute in a modest way to the peatiness of the whisky with which it is made.

"From our perspective there are more important things than price and in my view there is absolutely no doubt that the quality of Port Ellen malt is the best of that style"

MALTING
The first stage of whisky-making is malting, and this is the process that helps to define the essential character of Ardbeg more than any other. Traditionally, malting took place in individual distilleries, though today only a handful undertake on-site malting, with the others buying in malt prepared to their specification by commercial maltsters in large,

automated plants. In the case of Ardbeg, malt is acquired from the local Port Ellen Maltings, constructed in 1972/73 and owned by Diageo.

In distillery-based floor maltings, barley is steeped in water for two or three days, then spread on a malting floor, where rootlets develop as germination begins. So that the malt retains the sugars essential for fermentation, the partially germinated 'green malt', as it is known, is transferred to a kiln for around two days and dried over a fire or by jets of hot air, usually with some peat used in the furnace to impart flavour. The amount of peat introduced during kilning has a major influence on the character of the finished whisky. In modern, dedicated 'drum' maltings the processes remain broadly the same, but the scale is larger and a greater degree of automation is involved. Phenol levels of peating are measured in parts per million (ppm), and Ardbeg boasts one of the highest peating levels of any malt whisky.

Ardbeg is peated to a level of around 54ppm, and according to ex-distillery manager Stuart Thomson, "It's all about using a phenol level that complements your ultimate spirit. It's not simply about high phenols. I always felt that Ardbeg at between 45-55ppm best complemented the final product." Bill Lumsden adds "It can range from 45-65 as is it very difficult to achieve consistency at this level. I do have another supplier on the mainland who can supply heavily peated malt but Diageo is committed to the future of Port Ellen Maltings. From our perspective there are more important things than price and in my view there is absolutely no doubt that the quality of Port Ellen malt is the best of that style. Nobody quite does it like Port Ellen."

Former Ardbeg manager Iain Henderson recalls that when Allied Distillers were operating the site between 1989 and 1996 "All the malt came from Port Ellen Maltings, and we maintained a phenol level of 45-50ppm, though Port Ellen struggled to make 50ppm. I thought it was essential to maintain the peating level at that if we were to maintain the whisky's character." However, in the days when Ardbeg produced its own malt, peating levels were usually much higher. Ex-master blender Robert Hicks notes that "In the days of the old floor maltings, the peating level of Ardbeg was up to 80 or even 90 ppm. It was like creosote – very much tarry rope. At that point it was the most pungent and powerful whisky in the world."

"If you got the peat shed full in the summer you could peat the malt properly, but sometimes you'd just about end up burning turf! So the level of peating could vary considerably"

Mickey Heads notes that "It is important to have the correct phenol level on the malt, as 60-65 per cent is lost during the mashing and distillation processes." Ardbeg operated two separate maltings, with two malting floors in each, known as East and West, and was the last distillery on the island to produce all its own malt up to 1972. Unusually, the maltings were not equipped with fans in the roof top pagodas, causing the peat 'reek' to permeate the malt for a longer period than at other distilleries.

Hamish Scott was manager at Ardbeg in the days when the floor maltings last supplied 100 per cent of the distillery's requirements, and he says "At that time there were 12 or 13 men working solely on the maltings. We used mainly English and Australian barley, not much came from Scotland, whereas today distillers tend to use as much British barley as they can get hold of. We had a total of 30 production staff, working on a four-shift cycle. The maltings worked from 8am to 5pm, but the kiln men worked on shifts, and the kiln operated 24 hours a day, seven days a week."

Cutting peat from the distillery's own peat banks or 'lots' was an essential task in the distilling calendar, with the peat usually being harvested manually. Hamish recalls that "If you got the peat shed full in the summer you could peat the malt properly, but sometimes you'd just about end up burning turf! So the level of peating could vary considerably. Even in the 1960s it was hard to get people to cut it, so I set up a mechanical peat cutting company, called Islay Peat Developments, which sold peat to Ardbeg." The maltings were closed in 1981 when Hiram Walker shut the distillery down, but the 'in-house' floor maltings had been supplemented since 1973 by around 12.5 per cent of bought-in malt, and this quantity increased to 15 per cent in 1974. It was sourced from Kilgour's commercial matings at Kirkcaldy in Fife.

Whether produced in the distillery or in dedicated malting plants, the dried malt is ground in a mill to produce 'grist,' and at Ardbeg, as at many distilleries, grinding takes place in an old Boby mill. Ardbeg's mill is thought to have been manufactured just before the First World War.

MASHING
Once grist has been produced, the process of mashing begins. During 'mashing' the grist is mixed with hot water in a mash tun. This is a circular, metal vessel, and since the 1960s, many distilleries have adopted 'Lauter' or 'semi-Lauter' tuns, made from stainless steel, and fitted with

revolving arms which stir the mash gently. Ardbeg's mash house is fitted with a 16-feet, 'semi-Lauter' tun. Unusually, the modern, stainless steel semi-Lauter tun at Ardbeg is fitted into the characterful, cast iron base of its predecessor.

Bill Lumsden notes that "The old fashioned plough system that used to be installed at Ardbeg mashed up the mashbed. Once you have mashed it you want to leave it and very gently have your lauter gear rotating through it just to ease the drainage. Otherwise you force lots of solids through the plates as well. If you get a very cloudy wart, the particle, particularly the fatty acids, will suppress the formation of fruity esters which is not what you want. You want crystal clear wort which is good for spirit character." In the mash tun the starch in the grains is converted into a variety of sugars by enzymes within the grains, and the sugar goes into solution in the hot water, to be drained off through the base of the mash tun. This liquor is called 'wort'. The husks of the malt create a 'bed' in the bottom of the mash tun, through which the sugary wort can drain.

> *The temperature is crucial, for if it is too hot, it will kill the enzymes, and if it is too cool extraction will be limited*

Usually, three waters or 'extractions' are used for mashing. The first water, which is the third water from the previous mash, is heated to 63C or 64C, then mixed with the grist. The temperature is crucial, for if it is too hot, it will kill the enzymes, and if it is too cool extraction will be limited. This is drained off, then the second water is sprayed onto the mash at around 75C and the remaining sugars in the wort are drained off. To ensure there are no useable sugars left in the mix, a third water, called 'sparge' is then sprayed on, at around 85C, and this is transferred to a tank, to be used as the first water of the next mash.

According to mashman and stillman Ruaraidh MacIntyre ('Mackie') "The mashing temperature at Ardbeg is between 63.5 and 64 degrees, with the water going in at 68 degrees. The temperature of the grist brings it down to 64. It's a four and a half tonne mash and the mashing process lasts for seven and a half hours. The temperature is critical. We do 15 mashes a week at most. Lagavulin can do 25, because they have more washbacks and more stills. The same mash tun we have here at Ardbeg could do nearly twice as much if we had more washbacks and a second pair of stills!"

Once mashing is complete, the husks and other solids remaining in the mash tun - known as 'draff' - are removed, and as they are high in protein they are often sold as cattle food. Meanwhile, the wort passes through a heat exchanger to reduce its temperature to below 20C, which is necessary in order to prevent the yeast being killed off immediately during fermentation.

FERMENTATION
From the heat exchanger, the wort is pumped into a number of 'washbacks,' traditionally made from Oregon pine or larch wood, but now frequently constructed of stainless steel. At Ardbeg, tradition is maintained, with the tun room containing three Oregon pine and three larch washbacks, each with a capacity of 23,500 litres. The use of wooden washbacks is said to add a 'waxiness' to the character of the spirit ultimately produced. Distillery manager Mickey Heads explains that "It is virtually impossible to

sterilise wooden washbacks completely, so there is a small amount of bacteria left which gives a malolactic type fermentation, and results in a waxy note in the whisky."

As the wort enters the washback, a measured amount of yeast is added.

"In the mash house there's a control panel telling me all the temperatures and what's happening everywhere, but it's not computer-controlled, I'm controlling it, I'm making all the decisions"

Yeasts survive for years in a dormant state, but in the presence of sugars, warmth, moisture and an absence of air, they multiply at an extraordinary rate. They consume the sugars in the wort, converting it into alcohol and carbon dioxide. At this point the wort becomes 'wash'. The reaction during fermentation is violent, with the temperature increasing to around 33°C . The wash froths dramatically, and mechanical 'switchers' revolve over the surface, breaking the foam and preventing the wash from overflowing. The increasing temperature and rising alcohol level cause the yeast multiplication to slow down after some twelve hours, and results in a considerable increase in the amount of bacteria present, principally lactobacillus. There follows a period of bacterial fermentation, which is important for the development of flavour compounds and the degree of acidity in the wash. Longer fermentations produce a more acidic wash, which reacts beneficially with the copper in the wash still, producing a cleaner, more complex spirit.

Neil Johnston ('Philco') notes that "At Ardbeg we do 50 to 55 hour fermentations. The older the wash is, the easier it goes through the stills.

It doesn't stick to the heating pans and it distils more quickly." On each shift at Ardbeg one operator runs the mashtun and washbacks while the second controls the stills. James Gillespie ('The Gow') says that "In the mash house there's a control panel telling me all the temperatures and what's happening everywhere, but it's not computer-controlled, I'm controlling it, I'm making all the decisions. But it does make it easier to look after."

By the time fermentation is complete, the wash contains eight per cent alcohol, acidity has increased, and around 80 per cent of the solids in the wash have been converted into alcohol, carbon dioxide and new yeast cells. The remaining 15 per cent of solids pass over with the wash into the wash still, ready to be distilled.

DISTILLATION

Distillation is the defining aspect of whisky-making. Up to this point, the production process has been broadly similar to brewing beer, but now the strength of the alcohol is dramatically raised in copper pot stills. The design of these stills is crucial in determining the style of spirit they produce, and very few distilleries ever tamper with their basic still format, replacing worn out stills with exact replicas.

Ardbeg has one pair of wide-necked stills, now heated by internal steam coils, but previously fired by coal. Former master blender Robert Hicks notes that "Around 1975 steam coils were fitted to the stills, which made the spirit more constant. When the stills were hand-fired, they were much harder to control precisely." The fires beneath the stills were originally manually fed by shovelling in coal, however, recalling his early days at Ardbeg, Alexander Woodrow ('Wardie') says, "When I was in there, the stills were coal-fired, but had automatic feeders. Before the automatic feeders were put in you would have had to control the stills with dampers and the doors – opening and closing them. It was much more difficult then."

The crucial skill is to know exactly when to start saving spirit, and when to stop, though in many modern distilleries, cut points are dictated by computer programme

Ardbeg's wash still was installed in 1989 and has a capacity of 18,279 litres, while the spirit still dates from 2000, and can hold 16,957 litres. However, stills are never completely filled, and the 'charges' for the wash and spirit stills at Ardbeg are 11,775 litres and 13,660 litres respectively. Stillman Alistair Johnston ('Asha') notes that "After about 15 years, we keep an eye on the stills because the copper gets thinner. We can check with ultrasonic equipment to know how thin it is. The wash still is nearly 15 years old now, but the spirit still is much newer. I have heard rumours about putting another pair of stills in, but nothing has come of that so far."

The distillation process begins when the wash is pumped into the first or 'wash still', and is brought to the boil. The boiling liquid forms foam which ascends the neck of the still, and the stillman adjusts the heat to make sure the foam does not reach the top of the still and 'carry over' into the condenser. After a short while the foam subsides and the operator can turn up the heat and 'drive off' the spirit as vapour until the strength of the liquid left in the still (about 60 per cent of the original charge) has fallen to about one per cent alcohol by volume (abv) on the hydrometer, around 0.1 per cent in the still.

This is called 'pot ale' and is transferred to the distillery's effluent plant.

The vaporised spirit driven off the stills must be condensed back into liquid form, and this takes place either in modern 'shell and tube' condensers or in 'worm tubs.' Shell and tube condensers are tall, copper drums filled with dozens of narrow-bore copper pipes, through which cold water runs. The spirit vapour enters the drum and condenses on the cold, copper pipes. The worm tub is a coiled, copper pipe of diminishing diameter, set in a deep vat of cold water outside the still house. Until the 1970s, all distilleries used worm tubs, but today only around a dozen Scottish distilleries still employ them. Ardbeg dispensed with its worm tubs back in 1960.

The liquid produced by the wash still is called 'low wines,' and is pumped into a 'low wines receiver' before passing into the second, 'low wines' or 'spirit' still, along with the 'top and tail' (foreshots and feints) of the previous spirit distillation. The liquid is boiled in the same way as in the first distillation, but with two significant differences. The first spirits to come off, known as 'foreshots,' are high strength (around 75-80 per cent abv), pungent and impure, and are directed to a separate receiver tank, while the later spirits, known as the 'aftershots' or 'feints,' are also unpleasant in aroma and flavour, and join the foreshots. Both are added to the next batch of low wines for re-distillation.

Only the 'middle cut' of the run from the spirit still is directed to the 'intermediate spirit receiver' to be filled into casks, and the 'cut points' vary from distillery to distillery. The crucial skill is to know exactly when to start saving spirit, and when to stop, though in many modern distilleries, cut points are dictated by computer programme.

This is not the case at Ardbeg, however, as 'The Gow' explains. "The stills are even more 'hands on' than the mashing. All the cuts are made manually. I think people out there who drink the whisky like the fact that it's made by people, not by computers." 'Philco' adds "I like the fact we have manual cut points still and it takes a degree

We had to alter the length of the run to make sure we got the peatiness but not the nasty stuff, so it was a balancing act to get it right

of skill to run the stills properly. Nobody I know would just like to click a mouse to start a computer programme. You don't care what's happening if that's what you're doing. Fortunately, everybody we've spoken to in the company says they want it to stay the way it is." The spirit run from both stills pass through a locked brass box with a glass front, called a 'spirit safe,' inside which are glass jars containing hydrometers. If the stills are being run manually, the stillman manipulates handles on top of the safe to fill these jars and uses the hydrometers to measure the spirit's strength. When the optimum strength is achieved, he turns another handle and begins to save the middle cut. The same practice is observed when the feints begin to flow, and the stillman comes 'off spirit.' This mix of 'pure spirit' and impurities, or 'congeners', is different in every distillery, and plays a vital role in determining the character of the individual spirit. 'Asha' says "In the old days they used to mix water with the spirit in the spirit safe, instead of using a hydrometer, and if it wasn't clear it wasn't ready to cut from foreshots."

According to Mickey Heads, "At Ardbeg we run for ten minutes on foreshots. That way you get sweetness, with phenolics in the background. You are getting more esters at the start of the spirit run by not running foreshots for too long. The operatives are instructed to time for 10 minutes once the spirit has entered the safe and is settled down to its normal run speed. The strength is pretty constant at around 74% abv, and the temperature varies from 20°C in summer to as low as 6-7°C in winter. The strength can vary slightly according to the original and final gravity of the fermented wash, so, with good quality barley and a higher original gravity and good final attenuation, you will get a higher strength distillate."

Recalling earlier days, Robert Hicks points out that "The cuttings points were governed not by strength but by time. At Hiram Walker we looked at the actual flavours, not just how things had traditionally been done. The peat in Ardbeg comes through at the tail end of the main run, and we had to make sure we kept that peat flavour in as we adjusted cutting points. We had to alter the length of the run to make sure we got the peatiness but not the nasty stuff, so it was a balancing act to get it right.

Stuart Thomson says that "When Glenmorangie took over the distillery, Ed Dodson came over from Glen Moray in Elgin to get the place up and running again before I was appointed manager, and he took the decision to slow down the speed of distillation, to run the stills slower. The resulting spirit was more delicate and subtle. The boys will tell you that in the past the wash still had been filled half way up the neck. That's going to affect the quality, as there is less impact in the spirit against the copper, and there's a chance some of the wash won't even be distilled."

'Wardie' adds that "Now they use two lots from the wash still and one from the spirit still to make a charge. Previously, they would run the wash still off in three hours by bashing it through, but now they do it in around four hours."

"The wash still generally takes three hours to run," notes 'Philco,' "and with the spirit still, you fill it, put the steam on for 30 minutes to get it running. You then run it for ten minutes on foreshots, then four and a half hours 'on spirit,' as we call the middle cut, and finally three and a half hours running on feints."

"Ardbeg has a sweetness and also a powerful smoky, salty flavour," according to Mickey Heads. "This is due to a combination of the tall stills with a large surface area giving more copper contact, and the purifier which makes the spirit lighter, with a fruity sweetness." The spirit is greatly influenced by the presence of this purifier (almost unique to Ardbeg), which is fitted to the end of the lyne arm which leads from the top of the spirit still towards the condenser. As Stuart Thomson explains, "The lighter alcohols travel along the top of the lyne arm, while the heavier ones go along the bottom of the arm and are captured in the pot of the purifier. With the purifier, the whisky is nearly triple-distilled and this makes the spirit more delicate."

'Asha' says "The heavier spirit going over the neck of the still goes through the purifier and back into the still to be redistilled. That way you're not getting such heavy spirit," while 'The Gow' adds that "The purifier on the spirit still makes the spirit sweeter." Glenmorangie's master distiller Dr Bill Lumsden says "The purifier is undoubtedly what gives Ardbeg its fruity, floral sweetness, and gives complexity to the spirit."

The spirit still is run until its contents are around 0.1 per cent abv, and this waste residue is known as 'spent lees.' The product from the spirit still is usually referred to as 'new make' or 'clearic,' and is a clear liquid which is reduced with water from its natural strength (between 69.5 per cent and 70.5 per cent at Ardbeg) to around 63 or 64 per cent abv prior to filling into casks, as this is considered the optimum maturation strength. In terms of annual output, just under one million litres of spirit were produced in 2007, while the 2008 target is to top the million mark.

The influence of maturation in the creation of good whisky is immense, and some authorities consider that whisky acquires up to 80 per cent of its final character in the cask

MATURATION
Once the spirit has been produced, external influences play a vital role in determining just how it will look, smell and taste when it is bottled in several years' time. The influence of maturation in the creation of good whisky is immense, and some authorities consider that whisky acquires up to 80 per cent of its final character in the cask.

At Ardbeg some 98 per cent of new spirit is filled into ex-Bourbon barrels, and warehouseman Andrew Mullen ('Drew') observes that "We mainly fill into first and second refill Bourbon casks [capacity of 185 litres], with a few 'hoggies' [hogsheads, with a capacity of approximately 250 litres] and Sherry butts [capacity of approximately 500 litres] now and again." Stuart Thompson declares "I always felt that Ardbeg in many ways was better in a second fill cask. The first fill will give you more of the sweetness and tannins, and second time around you get more aldehytes, which means that you get more cereal, floral notes – hay, roses and chrysanthemums."

Speaking of the Hiram Walker and Allied Distillers' days, Robert Hicks recalls that "Virtually all the spirit being produced at Ardbeg was filled into ex-Bourbon barrels, as Hiram Walker was a 'barrel' company. They were usually first and second fill. Too much first fill wood tends to overpower a blend. I would say we were filling into a mix between good and 'decent' wood. We could always get plenty of casks from

Dunnage warehouses have fewer temperature variations due to their stone and slate roof construction, and are usually considered by distillers to be the best kind of warehouses for maturing their choicest spirit

the USA, as we had a deal with Makers Mark, so we never had to use bad wood."

While many distilleries now use computerised plastic 'bar codes' stapled to casks in order to identify their provenance, Stuart Thomson notes that "Glenmorangie, Glen Moray and Ardbeg all use stencilling instead of bar codes. Bar codes can get knocked off, and it's much easier to see the details of a stencil when you're unloading and stowing casks than it is to have to keep getting down and peering at a bar code." 'Wardie' points out that "We try to spread the casks around so we don't have all one year's production in one warehouse, just in case there's a fire, but we're pretty short of space, and basically we put newly-filled casks in wherever stuff comes out and leaves a gap."

The type of warehouses in which the spirit is stored and the location of those warehouses are also factors which influence the maturing spirit. During maturation there is evaporation of

ethanol and water, and the ingress of oxygen through the cask. The amount of bulk loss varies according to temperature and humidity levels, as does the speed of maturation. In a warehouse with a high level of humidity a greater amount of ethanol is lost than water, so the strength decreases. Conversely, low levels of humidity lead to a greater loss of water, and a consequent increase in strength. The environment of Scotland is comparatively cool and humid, so strength falls during maturation, while the liquid loss or 'angels' share' of evaporation is around two per cent per annum.

Traditional dunnage warehouses, usually constructed of stone, with an earth or cinder floor, feature casks stacked three high on wooden runners. Due to constraints of space, large, multi-storey warehouses have been constructed in more recent times. They are fitted with steel racks to hold casks, up to twelve rows high, closely packed together. For ease of operation, palletisation has also been introduced in many warehouses. Here casks are stacked not on their sides, as tradition has dictated, but on their ends on wooden pallets, up to six high.

Compared to modern, racked or palletised facilities, dunnage warehouses have fewer temperature variations due to their stone and slate roof construction, and are usually considered by distillers to be the best kind of warehouses for maturing their choicest spirit. Racked warehouses tend to be prone to greater seasonal fluctuations of temperature, but there are also temperature differences between casks stored close to the ground and those stored near to the roof. This is because maturation is fastest in the warmest area of a warehouse, which is invariably the highest part. According to 'Douga' "In the bottom three or four stows the temperature remains pretty constant, but it varies a lot up the racks. You can feel it change as you climb up."

There is an ongoing debate about whether the location of the warehouses affects maturing spirit, with one school of thought insisting there is no detectable difference between spirit matured, for example, by the sea on Islay, and that transported to the mainland for maturation in the Central Belt of Scotland. However, those closely associated with Ardbeg over the years

"For me, where it's matured has got to matter. The salt is in the air. The sea is just 100 metres away. The spray is hitting the walls of the warehouses at times, and you can taste it on your lips. You can feel the salty air in the warehouses."

have little doubt that this is not the case.

"The optimum place to mature Ardbeg is in a dunnage warehouse close to the sea," says Stuart Thomson. "You're going to get a lot more salt. The people that say it makes no difference are the people who want it to make no difference. Warehouse No 3 is 50 yards from the sea, so of course you're going to get an effect from all the salt air. Casks breathe. Where you mature the spirit has to be significant if you're using

dunnage warehouses. About 30 per cent of what Ardbeg matures goes into dunnage warehouses."

Mickey Heads is in agreement, saying "For me, where it's matured has got to matter. The salt is in the air. The sea is just 100 metres away. The spray is hitting the walls of the warehouses at times, and you can taste it on your lips. You can feel the salty air in the warehouses." 'Wardie' notes that "The effluent plant that now occupies warehouse No 1 was always one of the best for maturing whisky. It's right next to the sea, so maybe that's what did it. No 3's currently the best, and that's now the closest to the sea."

However, former Hiram Walker and Allied Distillers group distilleries manager Ian Miller recalls that "When production levels were high lots of the whisky made at Ardbeg was brought over to the mainland to mature. Once we had knocked down a lot of the old dunnage warehouses much of the spirit was being matured in racked warehouses. So you can argue that there was less difference between racked warehouses on the mainland and racked warehouses at the distillery once many of the old dunnage warehouses by the sea had gone. It's all a matter of opinion what happens when whisky is matured in different locations."

Barley, the primary ingredient used for making malt

*Peat is used to give the whisky its
distinctive, smoky character (opposite)*

Checking the temperature of the mash in the mashtun

Sterilising the wooden
washbacks (opposite)

Measuring the original gravity in the washback

Ardbeg's spirit still (opposite)

The "magical copper pot" purifier (page 112)

Newly-distilled, clear spirit

Unloading Bourbon casks which will be used to mature Ardbeg

123

Cask filling (opposite)

The courtyard, filling store and rear of the Old Kiln Café and Visitor Centre

Casks sleeping in a cool,
damp dunnage warehouse

THE BRAND

CHAPTER SIX

Having examined the heritage of Ardbeg, heard from the people who make the whisky and taken a look at how they make it, it is time now to turn to the whisky itself. Ardbeg will never be a 'middle-of-the-road' single malt for the uncommitted; it is a whisky that inspires great devotion in those who fall for its distinctive, peaty charms. As we shall see, it is marketed in a variety of expressions that reflect the spirit's fascinating provenance and diversity.

Ardbeg's global brand director Hamish Torrie joined Glenmorangie plc in March 1999, having previously worked for The Macallan in the formative period of its establishment as a single malt whisky brand. "The shape of the Ardbeg bottle and look of the label had already been set," he recalls. "Having finally got production back to the level of output recorded by Alfred Barnard (in the 1880s!) at around one million litres of alcohol, we have the scope to theoretically double sales in the next decade. But as we all know, malt whisky is a long term play, so who knows what will happen? Suffice to say that personally I believe Ardbeg should always be a niche brand in a very niche category. We bounce ideas around as a collective between Marketing and Production with many of the ideas gestating for three to four years before coming to fruition. For example it took about one and a half to two years to put the marketing plan together for Serendipity, and considerably longer for the Double Barrel."

Central to Ardbeg's core range is the ten-year-old bottling, though when Glenmorangie plc took over Ardbeg in 1997 there were significant gaps in the stock portfolio due to the distillery's previous periods of closure, and so the first expression launched by Glenmorangie was, of necessity, a 17-year-old. Glenmorangie's head of distilling and whisky creation Dr Bill Lumsden says "It's been a real challenge to eke out the stocks, to maintain quality and quantity given the bizarre stock situation we had inherited. The level of peating was all over the place, particularly in the older stock, but then you tend to find that in stock that comes from distilleries that run

their own maltings. It is not an exact science. Rather than see this as a problem we turned it round to our advantage to show the differing style of Ardbeg."

Warehouseman Douglas 'Dugga' Bowman adds "The oldest Ardbeg the company had was from 1965, just two casks which were bottled in 2006. Very few refill casks were used in the first year Glenmorangie owned Ardbeg, though I think second fill casks produce really good Ardbeg. We're currently filling around 50/50 first and refill casks. Anything special or different we try to keep in Number 3 warehouse. We've got casks of 1990 in there, and one is a fourth fill cask. You wouldn't think it would have been all that good, after so much use, but I think the whisky in it is fantastic."

Since 1997, Glenmorangie has had to be very creative with Ardbeg releases and this has gone hand in hand with some creative marketing. Hamish Torrie and Bill Lumsden joke about the Ardbeg marketing budget, but in truth very little has had to be spent on marketing the brand although clearly a great deal of thought goes into every bottling before it is released. Consequently, each expression seems to have its own interesting story, a few of which are related below.

Ardbeg 17-Year-Old (1997)
40.0% ABV

The first expression launched by Glenmorangie contained stock distilled under the previous Hiram Walker regime, and it was during this time the 'Kildalton' experimentation with varying peating levels was taking place (see Kildalton below). The 17-year-old was a comparatively lightly-peated Ardbeg, revealing a more delicate side to the spirit, unmasked by heavy phenol levels. It is ironic that whisky produced by Hiram Walker, who have received a great deal of criticism from aficionados for closing the distillery, has been responsible for converting so many drinkers to the delights of Ardbeg. Even among the distillery workers, the 17-year-old is generally favoured.

Provenance 1974 (1998/9)
55.8% ABV/55.6% ABV

Stuart Thomson recalls that when Glenmorangie took over Ardbeg "We actually found lots of gems, and some of the best were from 1974 and were bottled as Provenance. I can honestly say it's the best whisky I've tasted in my life. The subtlety was superb. It was delicate, smooth and honeyed, and with time you'd lost some of the phenols. Less than 100 casks went into it, giving 10,000 to 12,000 bottles. We did two batches, both from 1974, and half of the bottles were sold in the UK and half in the USA. There is no doubt that in 1974 there was a good wood policy and yet it is only in the last few years that the importance of the wood has been fully appreciated."

Ardbeg Ten Years Old (2000)
46.0% ABV

The core ten-year-old expression was finally released in 2000 using stock produced while Allied Distillers owned Ardbeg. This is a more 'gutsy' whisky than the 17-year-old, with a significantly higher phenol level. It was not necessarily matured in the most rigorously-selected casks, indicating how Ardbeg may have tasted in earlier incarnations.

According to Ardbeg's website, "Ardbeg Ten Years Old is a very special bottling for the Ardbeg distillery as it is the first non-chill filtered whisky in the Ardbeg range. Chill filtering isn't a bad thing, in fact it created real consistency of product when the whisky industry was a little more 'hap-hazard' than it is today. Ardbeg Ten Years Old is whisky with none of the goodness taken out and as good as straight from the cask."

From July 2008 the new Ardbeg Ten Years Old will be phased in, comprising spirit produced and matured entirely under the Glenmorangie regime. Bill Lumsden says "As far as humanly possible I've tried to recreate the same style for the new ten-year-old. It's heavily peated, of course, done to 50/65ppm at Port Ellen Maltings, and the quality of wood we've filled the spirit into is better than in the old days."

Ardbeg 1977 (2001)
46.0% ABV (2,400 bottles)

"I really can't find enough superlatives to describe this fantastic whisky. Rich, creamy, fudgey, smooth and smoky. Yum! Far and away the best peaty whisky I've ever had the privilege to drink. Some Ardbeg consumers love the 1974 and some the 1978, some even love the 'Very Young' above all others. Personally, I can't see past the 1977….and so the debate rages on!" Bill Lumsden

Lord of the Isles (2001)
46.0%ABV

In 2001 Ardbeg launched its greatly-admired 25-year-old Lord of the Isles expression, which was closer in style to the 17-year-old than the ten-year-old, and ultimately contained a percentage of 'Kildalton' spirit, contributing to its famously mellow character.

According to Hamish Torrie, "We owned the Lord of the Isles trademark, and if you've got something as distinctive as that you really have to use it. Somerled was the first Lord of the Isles and one of his successors was Dougal, so you get Clan Dougal and then Macdougall, and it was the Macdougalls who founded Ardbeg in 1815.

"The launch of Lord of the Isles was held in the National Museum in Edinburgh, the reason being that the presentation box for the whisky was inspired by the Monymusk Reliquary, an 8th century box which held relics of St Columba, the second rarest thing linking to the Lord of the Isles. The box was paraded before the troops at the battle of Bannockburn in 1314 by Robert the Bruce to get God on their side.

"We've been eking out stocks since its launch in 2001, and essentially it's 1974 and '75 whisky going into it, plus some 1976 when we had it. So the most recent bottlings are actually 30 years plus."

Bill Lumsden adds that "It's been a core part of the

range using some of the more delicate whiskies, and people love it. When we've opened a bottle at whisky events people congregated to taste it like bees round a honey pot. People have even wanted the empty bottle!"

Ardbeg 21-year-old (2001)
56.3% ABV

"I'm a modest guy," declares Stuart Thomson "but the 21-year-old we came out with was my biggest achievement in terms of picking casks. I chose six casks from 1979 and six from 1980, and samples were sent over to Glenmorangie's head office in Broxburn. Ultimately they were blended by Bill Lumsden and Rachel Barrie and they produced a fabulous whisky."

Ardbeg Committee Reserve (2002)
55.3% ABV (3,000 bottles)

Following the establishment of the Ardbeg Committee in 2002 a special, limited quantity bottlings was released and made available exclusively to Committee members. This release went on to demonstrate the strength of Ardbeg's following, and provided an indication to Ardbeg's owner Glenmorangie of the value of establishing a strong link with their consumers.

Uigeadail (2003)
54.2% ABV

Uigeadail was launched in 2003 as a cask strength addition to the Ardbeg line up, and features a mixture of 1993 whisky matured in ex-Bourbon casks and older, former oloroso Sherry casks.

"Michael Jackson was at the launch of Lord of the Isles," recalls Bill Lumsden, "and he said to me almost as if he were hypnotising me 'It's very nice, but I like my Ardbegs 'MUCKY, MUCKY AND DIRTY,' and so a 'mucky dram' emerged.

"This led us to Uigeadail. It was a response to Michael's comments, but I wanted to create something different from the others in the range

anyway. There was a higher use of Sherry wood than in most expressions, and we have filled a lot of Sherry casks for future Uigeadails because the Sherry is part of its style. It is an ongoing part of the core range."

"It was very important to be able to root the name of the expression on Islay," declares Hamish Torrie. "Uigeadail is the loch from which Ardbeg takes its water. It's a challenging whisky and the pronunciation of its name is a challenge too. We're fine with that; it generates interest."

Very Young Ardbeg - For Discussion (2003)
58.9% ABV

"Necessity is the mother of invention," declares Hamish Torrie. "We have to be creative with Ardbeg as we do not have large stocks to work with. Hence the Very Young Ardbeg - For Discussion. The idea was to put it to the Committee and to create discussion. You then get endorsement and that gives you legitimacy. The idea was to offer 1997 Ardbeg (the fist of our distillation) just to let people know we were taking care of it and going in the right direction. Labelled 'For Discussion,' the release encouraged feedback and gave enthusiasts the opportunity to sample and express their views on the new owner's six-year-old produce."

The Peaty Path to Maturity (2004-2008)

Following the success of 'Very Young Ardbeg - For Discussion,' a revolutionary concept was instigated, based on releasing a series of expressions from the same year to mark the ongoing process of maturation in the spirit distilled under Glenmorangie's first full year of ownership. Using quirky names, the earliest release was 'Very Young' (58.3%ABV), which at six years old featured spirit produced in 1998. Thus the 'Peaty Path to Maturity' commenced.

With the subsequent bottling the consultative process continued to be encouraged, albeit not exclusively via the Committee. The following releases of 'Still Young' (56.2%ABV) in 2006 and 'Almost There' (54.1%ABV) in 2007 offered a unique insight into how a whisky can change and develop year on year.

As Hamish Torrie says, "We turned the idea of aged whisky on its head, smacked its bottom and sent Very Young Ardbeg out into the world. Because of the stock situation, invention and fun came about."

Committee consultation served not only to generate a great deal of feedback from Members for the company, but also, as Jackie Thomson says, "It's great for the Committee members to have the luxury of being able to compare the spirit as it matures. The 'For Discussion' bottling was brilliant. It made people feel really involved."

Kildalton (2004)
57.6% ABV

2004 not only saw innovation in the form of 'Very Young,' but also a limited release of 1,300 bottles of Ardbeg Kildalton, dating from 1980. Robert Hicks was intimately involved in the production of Kildalton, and explains just what it was and why it was distilled.

"During the period from 1978 to December 1980 there were continuous experiments run at the distillery using various sources of malted barley and varying levels of peating, from 100 per cent unpeated plain malt to 100 per cent traditionally peated Ardbeg malt.

"The concept was to maintain the distillery at maximum production in economic and distilling terms. If the distillery continued using 100 per cent traditional malt then there would be an unbalanced stock position in the future. The decision was then taken to use various sources and peating levels to have, in the long term, a malt whisky that encompassed the traditional level of phenols at one end of the spectrum (Ardbeg) and a more usable lightly unpeated malt (Kildalton) that could be used at a higher inclusion in blends without impacting on flavour.

"Experimentation at distilleries in Hiram Walker's time was relatively common, as can be seen by the use of Lomond style stills at Scapa, Glenburgie and Miltonduff and the many experiments tried at Glencadam.

"Very early in the experiment some distinct problems surfaced. The first being that without installing a separate receiver to collect the two very different styles of feints then the heavy phenol character obtained when using 100 per cent Ardbeg malt became readily apparent during the first following run using unpeated malt. This gradually lessened over subsequent runs until unpeated distillate was produced.

"The experiment was altered from using 100 per cent unpeated to using varying levels of unpeated to peated malt. This alteration then produced the second problem in that the mixing of the different styles of malt was not uniform. During each week's production the distillate could vary from similar to Ardbeg to nearly plain.

"These problems meant that over the experimental runs there was only a small amount of fully unpeated whisky produced and that the majority varied between 20 per cent and 75 per cent character and that this variance could be contained within one week's production. Distillate produced using non Ardbeg malt was coded Ardbeg Kildalton but the character of this varied from near traditional Ardbeg (90 per cent) to plain (0 per cent).

The distillery ran this experiment until December 1980. Due to the 'whisky lake' that became apparent in the late 1970s and early '80s, Ardbeg ran 100 per cent unpeated malt from January to March 1981 when it closed."

According to Bill Lumsden "It was not completely unpeated but as near as damn it. If you assume bottled Ardbeg has circa 25-30ppm phenol in it, which is roughly half what's originally in the malted barley, then the Kildalton had about 4ppm. You can measure the phenols in the whisky itself and we measure by the industry standard 'indophenols,' the colorimetric method, although some use HPLC which artificially inflates the reading."

Hamish Torrie recalls "It has an amazing delicacy to it and it sold like hot cakes."

Ardbeg 1965 (2006)
42.1%ABV

The following year saw the distillery offer its oldest and most expensive bottling up to that point in the shape of Ardbeg 1965. Bill Lumsden notes that "We have not had to re-rack much but we did have to re-cask the mighty 1965 vintage as the two casks we had were leaking and there was very little whisky left in them. We had to rescue it and had the two re-racked into one single refill, refill, refill Sherry butt. I was not looking for influence, just a container to save this precious liquid."

Hamish Torrie is proud of the promotional campaign for the bottling which included a 'viral' which was a parody of the Chanel Egoiste advert of 1988/9. "The Chanel ad is about the extreme envy felt towards one shuttered house in San Tropez that remains closed. In the Chanel add a bottle of Egoiste comes out, in our ad the 1965 came out."

Marketed as 'The Envy of Islay,' the viral can still be seen at www.ardbeg1965.com

Just 261 bottles of '1965' were released, and the beautifully-crafted 70cl bottle was presented in a glass case, along with a 5cl bottle for collectors to drink and actually experience the elusive, old spirit. Each bottle was fitted with a numbered, wax seal, and there was even a small amount of Islay sand used in the manufacture of the glass. The few retailers who were allocated stocks of Ardbeg 1965 were issued with pairs of white gloves to wear while handling the bottles, like museum curators with precious, ancient objects.

Ardbeg Double Barrel (2006)

If Ardbeg 1965 was the ultimate Ardbeg bottling in terms of age and retail price, then 'Double Barrel' took the concept of luxury presentation of fine and rare whisky to an entirely new level.

According to Hamish Torrie, "The initiative was conceived by us three or four years ago, before LVMH came along and purchased Glenmorangie. Inspired by the tradition of a shooting party, Ardbeg created a 'Double Barrel' gun case, crafted by a traditional gun case maker."

The case contains two single cask bottles of 1974 Ardbeg from three pairs of casks, so it is not all the same whisky in every bottle. Accompanying the rare spirit are eight sterling silver Hamilton & Inches drinking cups, a bespoke oak and sterling silver Omas pen, complete with detailed Ardbeg engraving, two hand-stitched leather-bound books – a 'Sampling Register' with full tasting notes of the 1974 cask bottlings and 'Double Barrel', a quirky miscellany of Ardbeg single malt and shooting traditions. Only 250 Double Barrels were released internationally, priced at £10,000.

Airigh Nam Beist (2007)
46.0%ABV

Uigeadail may have presented consumers with difficulties of pronunciation, but the 2007 release Airigh Nam Beist gave them an even bigger challenge.

Airigh nam Beist is the name of the second loch that provides Ardbeg's distillery water. It therefore performs a balancing role in supplying the water from Loch Uigeadail required by the distillery. Airigh Nam Beist (pronounced 'arry-nam-baysht') in Gaelic means 'shelter of the beast.' According to the packaging "No more fitting name could have been bestowed on such an eerie place; this is where - legend has it - something other-worldly lurks, lying in wait. So what measures can be taken to protect local and visitor alike? If you find yourself straying this way, then pray equip yourself with that traditionally reliable antidote to sheer terror - the stiff drink. A travelling man could ask for no better protection than a hip flask full of the strong stuff, namely Ardbeg`s Airigh Nam Beist. For it's truly a wee beastie of a dram - waiting to be released!"

Hamish Torrie say that "The aim is to have three different styles of Ardbeg rather than ages," while Bill Lumsden adds that "Airigh nam Beist was a homage to the old and very popular 17-year-old. We wanted something subtle, and lots of the first fill ex-Bourbon casks added creaminess and softness. It fitted in well with the 'standard' 10-year-old and the Christmas pudding-like Uigeadail style. The name came about as a result of myself, The Gow and Douga looking at a map of Islay spread out on the bonnet of a car, trying to find a name for the whisky! We followed down from Uigeadail and came to Airigh nam Beist, the deep dark mysterious, peat-laden loch from which the water is drawn."

Ardbeg Mor (2007)
57.3%ABV

Ardbeg's open day during the 2007 *Feis Ile* (Islay Festival of Malt and Music) saw the release of Ardbeg Mor which was designed to celebrate the tenth anniversary of the distillery's renaissance. Mor contained the equivalent of more than six bottles of 10 Years Old, but instead of being offered at the usual strength of 46% ABV, it was presented at a cask strength of 57.3% ABV. 1,000 bottles were released, and once more a Gaelic theme was present in the name, as Mor means 'big' or 'magnificent.'

Renaissance (2008)

In June 2008 the 'Peaty Path to Maturity' will be complete with the release of 'Renaissance' or 'We've Arrived'. Once again, 1998 stock which is now 10 years old will be used for the bottling, and according to Bill Lumsden "We may be horribly biased but it's an absolute cracker. I'm amazed by the incredibly, rich 'tropical fruit' type character I find in this whisky."

Single Casks

In addition to the expressions listed above there has been a steady flow of Ardbeg single cask bottlings since 1999. Stuart Thompson fondly recollects a number of outstanding releases:

"In July 2000 two (1976) Oloroso Sherry casks were picked to be hand filled - as an exclusive Ardbeg Committee bottling. On the Friday afternoon we had evaluated the casks and demonstrated how many bottles you would get from the casks for customs. On the Monday I sent the boys down to get the casks and to take them over to the filling store. One of the guys came up ten minutes later and said 'You won't believe this, one of the casks has totally emptied.' It had emptied over the weekend just like that. It had a 'worm hole' (which is a porous piece of wood) right in the bottom that had become more and more porous, so it had sat there for 25 years and just opened up in those three days. It was a beautiful, beautiful whisky, and it had probably emptied in about an hour. The lost cask was number 2393, so we had to select another cask to fill with and so we ended up with casks 2392 and 2394. Cask 2395 which went to Japan was superb as well. Then there was a 1972 bottling done for V.E.L.I.E.R, an Italian distributor, and that was fantastic whisky too."

> *Under the ownership of Glenmorangie, the sort of wood experimentation programme that has been so successful with the Glenmorangie single malt range has also been applied to Ardbeg. Mickey Heads says "We're filling batches into different types of cask by way of experimentation. Toasted oak, plain, new oak, wine casks. Just maybe 15 to 20 barrels of each."*
>
> *Stuart Thomson notes that "In my time at Ardbeg we experimented with French casks, including Burgundy, and there are six ex-claret casks in the warehouse, which we filled to see what would happen."*

Ten Years Old, first released in 2000 at 46% and 17-Year-Old first released in 1997 at 40%

Lord of the Isles

single Ardbeg islay malt scotch whisky

This rare old malt whisky is the supreme expression of ardbeg. it has been slowly matured in oak barrels for twenty five years and is non chill-filtered to retain maximum flavour. the lords of the isles ruled the western isles of scotland from their 'council isle' on islay from the 12th to the 15th century. the celtic, norse warlord, somerled, founder of the lordship dynasty through his three sons dugall, ranald and angus was thus the progenitor of the two great clans of macdonald and macdougall. the ardbeg distillery was founded on islay in 1815 by john macdougall.

distilled and bottled in scotland
ardbeg distillery limited
isle of islay, argyll, scotland

Various vintage Ardbegs: 1975 first released in 1998 at 43%, 1977 first released in 2001 at 46%, 1978 first released in 1997 at 43% and 1990 first released in 2004 at 55%

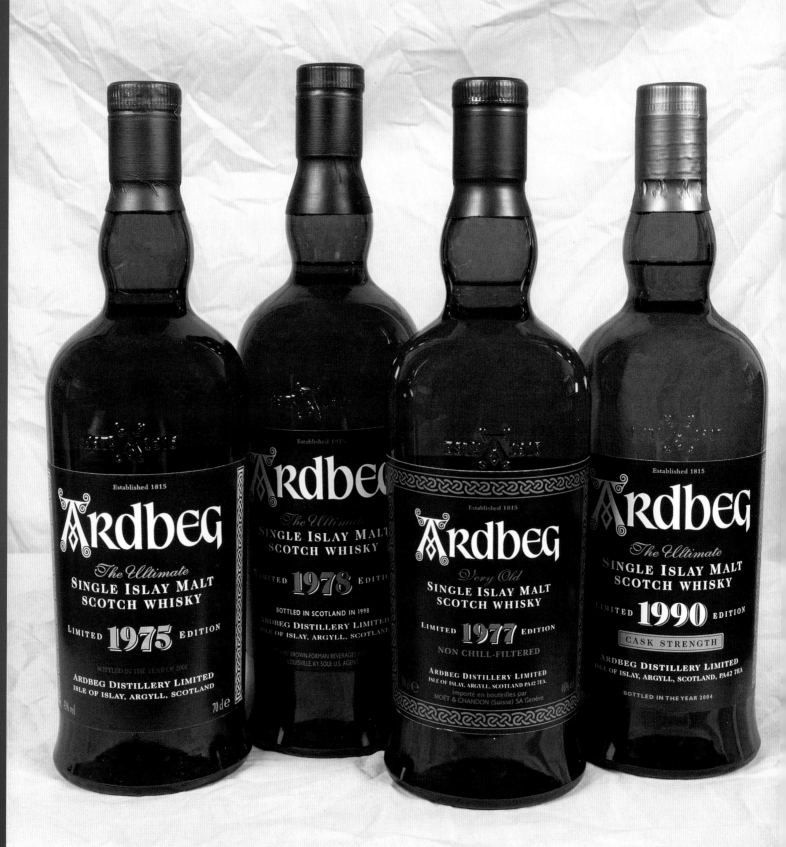

Various Committee bottlings: Single Casks 2392 and 2394, bottled in July 2000 and distilled in November 1976, together with the 21-Year-Old for the Committee bottled in 2001 from 12 casks distilled in 1979 & 1980

*Airigh nam Beist, first released in 2006 at 46%, distilled in 1990,
with Uigeadail, first released in 2006 at 54.2%*

Kildalton, released in 2004 at 57.6%. The lightly peated Ardbeg

The path to peaty maturity: Very Young released in 2004 at 58.3%, Still Young released in 2006 at 56.2% and Almost There released in 2007 at 54.1%. All distilled in 1998

Renaissance

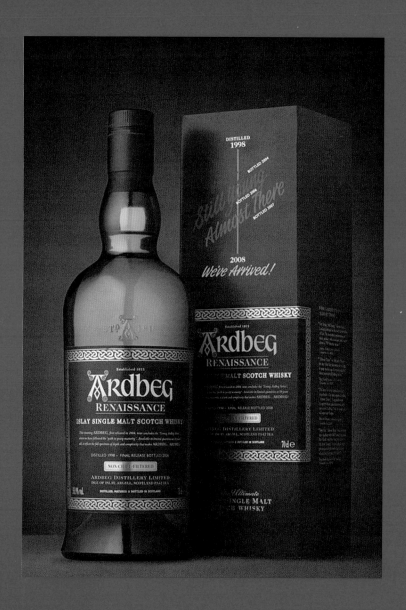

…'We've Arrived'

Managers Choice Single Cask 2391, bottled in June 1999 and distilled in November 1976.
The first and arguably the best single cask bottling by Glenmorangie

The differing labels used for Single Cask bottlings: Cask 4718 released in October 1999, distilled in December 1975, Cask 4701 released in March 2002, distilled December 1975 and Cask 4699 released in February 2006, distilled in December 1975

1965, released in 2005 at 42.1%. Vatted from two casks and bottled at 40 years old

ARDBEG, DISTILLED 1965

A very rare vatting of Islay Single Malt Whisky
drawn from two exceptionally old Ardbeg casks,
nos. 3678 and 3679. Bottled at cask strength in
2005 and non chill-filtered for maximum flavour

BOTTLE No: 085   OF 261

Double Barrel , released in 2007. Sold in pairs, each set is from two of six differing casks distilled in 1974

SERENDIPITY (2005)
40.0% ABV

While all other Ardbeg releases are the result of careful deliberation between production and marketing staff, based on stock availability and perceived 'gaps in the market,' one expression came about entirely by accident. One day in 2004 a member of staff in the blending facility at Glenmorangie's Broxburn headquarters mistakenly vatted a quantity of old Ardbeg with some 12-year-old Glen Moray.

As Hamish Torrie explains, "It was 16,000 bottles worth – it was a major problem at the time. As a marketeer I was tasked to get value out of what were essentially damaged goods. We could have blended it away, just putting small amounts into various blends, but the value of the stock was too great for that. It was 80 per cent Ardbeg, around 20 years old and more lightly peated, destined for the 17-year-old bottling, and 20 per cent 12-year-old Glen Moray.

"I thought why don't we just own up to what's happened and offer it to the Committee first to buy. The meaning of the word 'serendipity' had been explained to me by my father when I was a boy, and it stuck with me. It just seemed the perfect name for this whisky – making happy discoveries by accident.

"To deliberately fool people even further, the mailer for Serendipity was sent out to arrive on the doormats on 1st April 2005 (April Fool's Day) with the idea of keeping people guessing whether is was a genuine mistake. Was it true or was it a wind up? I consider this bottling to be one of those dream moments where a marketeer gets the opportunity to really prove his or her mettle ......very satisfying!"

THE EXPERIENCE

CHAPTER SEVEN

During the summer of 2006 I had dinner with fellow whisky writer Ian Buxton, who also runs the World Whiskies Conference. We were dining in the palatial surroundings of Edinburgh's Balmoral Hotel, with two wealthy and successful Russian whisky aficionados who were being entertained on their visit to Scotland by Ian. One was Rear Admiral Dr Grigory Korolkov and the other was his colleague Viktor Voskresenskiy. We drank vintage Port Ellen malt instead of wine with our meal, each course of which was accompanied by a lengthy and complex Russian toast, conducted according to a strict and unbending etiquette. Our hosts attached great importance to this.

During the meal Admiral Korolkov expressed his desire to acquire a bottle of Ardbeg 1965, which was officially sold out by this time. However, ever-resourceful, Ian promised to do his best to locate a bottle which, even then, retailed for rather more than £2,000. "Is this for your collection?" I enquired through the Russians' interpreter. When my question was translated the Admiral laughed and shook his head, raising an imaginary glass to his lips. "It is to drink," replied the interpreter, "he says whisky is to drink, not collect. It will be opened at his forthcoming 60th birthday party."

As Ian Buxton recalls, "Getting the whisky was quite a performance. All the obvious sources had sold out, but through senior contacts at the company's HQ I was able to establish that a very few bottles had been held in reserve 'for those and such as those.' Fortunately, a Russian nuclear submarine Admiral qualified and a bottle was obtained. This information was received as we drove round Edinburgh's city by-pass with the jubilant visitors, who promptly produced an American Express card and proceeded to consummate the deal over my mobile phone. Such is the lifestyle of the new Russians!" At around £70 per standard bar measure this made for some expensive birthday toasts, but then Ardbeg inspires a remarkable devotion among people who appreciate fine whisky – and have the deep pockets to indulge their enthusiasm.

There are many such examples of Ardbeg's iconic status, and warehouseman Douglas Bowman ('Douga') says "There was a German Ardbeg fan who was due to go on holiday to South Africa with his girlfriend a few years ago, but when he heard we were putting a new spirit still in he came here instead. He just sat watching the work for three days!

Emma McGechie, who works alongside Jackie Thomson in the visitor centre and Kiln Café and undertakes guided tours of the distillery, also has a story relating to the loyalty and good fellowship inspired by Ardbeg. "During the Gulf War one of our Ardbeg Committee members said a friend of his was an officer in the Navy and couldn't get his favourite Ardbeg, so we sent him a complementary bottle, with a card wishing him and the crew well. He was on board *Ark Royal*, and we didn't know if he'd get it. His name was Lieutenant Commander Paul Russell. Months later, he got in touch and said he'd received the bottle and that *Ark Royal* was sailing into Greenock on the Clyde, arranged for the ship to anchor just off Ardbeg and took us on a tour to say thank you. He anchored out there and 60 officers and men came ashore for distillery tours and just about bought up the shop!

"Then nine of us were taken out for a tour of *Ark Royal* and had dinner on board. We all had our survival suits on and we had to jump off the wee boat onto a ladder and climb up onto the deck. By mistake, Jackie gave the captain my body warmer as one of the gifts we took. A few days later I got a parcel back containing my eyeliner, lipstick, and all sorts of bits and pieces out of the pockets of the body warmer, including a credit agreement for my car. With it was a letter from the captain saying he would have kept the lipstick, but it wasn't his colour!"

Crucial to the development of Ardbeg as a whisky with an international cult status was the creation of the Ardbeg Committee. This was launched in 2002, and an explanatory leaflet was placed in each bottle's packaging, and an online presence was subsequently established. According to global brand director Hamish Torrie, "Five thousand people signed up in the first six months, and now we have around 38,000 in total.

"The Committee is certainly not a gimmick," he insists, "it's there to spread the word. We try to give members the 'inside track' wherever possible. We give them the first 'in' on any new expression we release. A Committee member once came up to me and said 'If you bottled air we'd buy it!'" Anyone signing up to become a Committee member receives regular Momentous Minutes mailshots, and by logging on at the website they are able to address the 'Chair' of the Committee, buy and sell whisky-related items, purchase Ardbeg whisky and branded goods, and even discover what the weather is like on Islay!

According to Emma McGechie "When Hamish and the other marketing people first came over they couldn't believe how many committees there were on Islay. For a small island, there was a sheepdog committee, a quilting committee, a poultry committee and so on. They decided to form an Ardbeg Committee and the newsletters are all written in committee-style language."

Jackie Thomson adds "Islay has a population of 3,000 people and 140 committees! In rural areas they are important. With the Ardbeg Committee we're taking something quintessentially Islay and opening it up to a wider audience. The Committee has been a great tool to allow Ardbeg to grow and flourish. The special Committee bottlings have instilled loyalty and have continued to tantalise people. The Committee members are very much part of the fabric of the place. They're the cornerstone of the brand."

According to Committee literature, "No matter how near or far, our members share a common purpose: to celebrate the reawakening of Ardbeg and dispense drams to those deprived of knowledge about The Ultimate Islay Malt Whisky."

Committee Rules 4, 5 and 6 are as follows:-

4. The Committee is established for the object of promoting the advancement of general knowledge and enjoyment of Ardbeg.

5. Responsibilities of membership are primarily to enhance the member's own quality of life through greater understanding and consumption of The Ultimate Islay Malt Whisky.
6. Moreover, members are expected to actively pursue a serious and altruistic duty: to bring others into the Ardbeg fold. The result of the collective effect of this is to increase worldwide consumption, thereby ensuring that the doors of Ardbeg Distillery shall never close again.

The Ardbeg Committee is just one way in which the whisky has been successfully promoted, and October 2002 saw the launch of the 'Beg to Differ' marketing campaign, designed to appeal to a broader range of drinkers as well as whisky aficionados. As Hamish Torrie notes "We avoided stereotypical whisky ads complete with visual clichés. We created a peculiar and arresting campaign which inextricably links day-to-day life on Islay with Ardbeg. As ever, everything Ardbeg says is rooted in truth, so our headlines were derived from the actual tasting notes of established whisky writers."

A feature of much of Arbeg's advertising material is Shortie, a Jack Russell terrier owned by a family which lives close to the distillery. Hamish Torrie describes the marketing of Ardbeg as "whimsical," noting that "Shortie is a symbol of our unorthodox approach to marketing Ardbeg. He has been part of what we do from the start. Being able to take that sort of approach comes from having real confidence in your product." The success of 'Beg to Differ' and other promotional programmes can be gauged by the fact that Ardbeg was the fastest growing malt whisky brand in the world between 1998 and 2004, and Glenmorangie Company Ltd has won more than 30 international marketing awards for Ardbeg since 1999.

Such is the passion engendered by all things Ardbeg that many Committee members and other aficionados are not content with drinking the spirit and interacting via the Arbeg website and through newsletters. An increasing number of them are ultimately finding their way to the inner sanctum, the distillery itself. According to Hamish Torrie, ""From the fans' point of view Ardbeg became a Mecca; the place to get to."

"I visited Islay last summer. Seven Finnish gentlemen spent a week there, in the good care of Christine Logan [who trades as 'The Lady of the Isles' and offers personalised visitor experience packages.] We went through all the operational distilleries and, of course, our first visit was to Ardbeg. We met Michael Heads and had a long chat and tour with him. For me it was a visit to the Holy Land. To see the people, places and machinery which manufacture my favourite whisky. Mickey had heard from Christine that I'm writing a whisky book so we might have received a special treatment from him. At the end of our tour we ended up at one of the warehouses and we tasted straight from the cask 1990 Bourbon and 1999 Madeira Ardbegs. Immaculate! And as we were led to Old Kiln Café for lunch, Mickey brought a bottle of 1975 cask 1375 and we had a wee dram of it too. Islay hospitality at its best! If the other members of my entourage weren't Ardbeg believers before, they surely are now.

I corresponded with Jackie and talked with her over the phone before our journey and she has always been helpful and easy to talk to. She takes superb care of the Old Kiln and still during the busiest lunch she has time for our never ending questions. Her warm smile and even warmer hug are amongst my best memories of Islay.

As our stay at Islay was ending, we visited Ardbeg once more, just to do some shopping and see the site one more time. We didn't know that Christine and Mickey had arranged something special for us. Mickey greeted us on the yard and presented us with a bottle of Ardbeg Airigh Nam Beist and told us to go to the pier, have a dram and reflect the feelings and experiences we've had during our stay on Islay. One could almost see the haziness in the eyes of big, bold men as we had our drams at the beautiful pier looking at the sea and the white warehouse with black block letters, ARDBEG."

Jarkko Nikkanen, Finland.

"I organise a trip to Islay for my club UBEL every spring during the Feis Ile. We are always very welcomed by dear Jackie. Last year we went up to Loch Uigeadail first, and down into the Old Kiln Café comes nine guys covered with dirt up to the knees and very thirsty, just before closing time. Nine Uigeadail's on the house (what else?), a couple of beers (per guy) and some lovely thick soup and fresh bread. The guys praised me as an excellent organiser, but it was all due to Jackie and her lovely staff. We love to come back every year.

Ingvar Andersson, Sweden

As Jackie Thomson says, "Coming to Islay is a grown up holiday. You've got to organise flights and ferries and so on. It says a lot about how intrepid people can be. It's not a casual thing you do on a day off." Upon arrival at Ardbeg distillery visitors are usually greeted in the visitor centre by Jackie or Emma McGechie, and offered a tour of the distillery. The degree of formality depends on how many people are visiting at the time, with Emma noting "Yesterday I took a tour round with just six people, and we took an hour and a half, because they were all so interested. Obviously you can't do that in summer when it's very busy."

Both Emma and Jackie weave their individual magic, and Frank Vernicuwe of Belgium was prompted to write in the visitors' book "The tour was led by a spirit fairy named Jackie. After a few sentences it was not an organised tour anymore, but someone sharing their passion with a few visitors." An anonymous and discerning member of the public also noted in the visitors' book "Excellent tour! Mrs Thomson is a babe!"

Hamish Torrie says "Jackie perfectly epitomises the modern, unorthodox approach we go for, combined with fantastic heritage," and Bill Lumsden adds "Stuart and Jackie had a youthful approach compared to the usual distillery manager and his wife. They brought a vibrant, young aspect to the job, and they were both excellent with visitors."

"The visitor centre and café set up was on the agenda right from when Glenmorangie bought Ardbeg," declares Hamish. "The distillery is at the end of the road, so to get people to come that far you needed something to seduce them. It started with coffee and a bun, but its reputation grew and it became a full-blown eaterie. It's given Islay a bistro-style venue, and it's now *the* place to eat on Islay.

"Mary in the kitchen is fantastic – her cooking is to die for. Her clootie dumpling is now famous all over the world." This being Islay, Mary is the aunt of Ardbeg's mashman Archie McKechnie ('Yogi'.) According to Emma, "The café can do 180 lunches a day in the summer. It's a bit like catering for a wedding every day! People may have to wait for up to 40 minutes in a queue for a table, but they don't seem to mind."

Not all Jackie and Emma's work is 'front of house,' and Emma says "There's always something to do here, even in January. When there are new bottlings we send out flyers to Britain, Germany, Sweden and other countries. Then the orders come in, and it's all done from here. It's just us here wrapping and posting them. All the post goes out through Florence at the post office in Port Ellen, and it goes off the island by plane. The plane has a weight restriction, so sometimes if we have a lot of bottlings to post they can't all go out in one go! The interest for orders has snowballed. We try to download them from the internet every day to keep up.

"I think Committee members believe it comes from some huge, central warehouse, but actually we do it all. Jackie wanted everything to come from the distillery, and it helps the local post office, sending it all out from here. We all chip in. If necessary, I'll clean the café floor and the kitchen floor at the end of the day and some of the kitchen staff will come out and help us to pack. Once we were short of a warehouseman and a truck had to be unloaded, so I went up into the truck and rolled out the casks, down onto the sponge for the boys to put into the filling store."

All the dedication and hard work of the Ardbeg team have been rewarded by increased sales of whisky, a greatly enhanced international profile for the spirit and its distillery and the establishment of a visitor destination of great distinction. Happily, the transformation effected at Ardbeg has not gone unnoticed in the wider world of whisky.

"Through the years, I and my friend Niklas have become very close friends with Stuart Thomson. It all started with the release of the Ardbeg 1972 (bottled for Sweden), a bottle which we didn't get our hands on when it was released in our country. We started to make phone calls to Ardbeg and was promised another bottle of 1972. Several phone calls later we hade started to connect to Stuart and Jackie.

We have held three tastings with Stuart as a guest, two of them were arranged for more than 70 people each, but the third was on Stuart's own initiative. He called us and wondered if he could come for a tasting – with only five days notice in advance. Of course, we arranged that, but as a small more informal tasting for about 20 people. This summer we invited Stuart to Varberg for a week, a week which we spent enjoying good whisky, football and friendship."

Jorgen Andersson, Sweden

Although the summer months are inevitably the busiest for the Ardbeg visitor centre and café team, the week-long annual Islay Festival of Malt & Music – *Feis Ile* – staged each May, sees several thousand devotees make their pilgrimage to Islay, and there is barely a bed to be found on the entire island.

Each of Islay's working distilleries has a dedicated open day, with Ardbeg usually taking the final Saturday of the Festival. In 2007, a number of local musicians played during the day to help maintain an upbeat, vibrant atmosphere during atrocious weather. One act was 'Eddie & Friends,' whose members boasted a remarkable distilling pedigree between them. The line up consisted of vocalist Eddie Brown, a painter who was involved in the distillery refurbishment in 1997, his fiddle-playing daughter Rebecca, accordionist David Adams, who worked as a warehouseman at Laphroaig for 27 years, and banjo player Donnie McKinnon, formerly brewer at Lagavulin, where he was employed for 39 years, and is now owner of the Islay Sea Safari company, which also takes people on sea tours of the distilleries.

Many of the island's distilleries produce an exclusive Festival release, and the 2007 Festival saw the appearance of Ardbeg Mor (see Chapter Six). In keeping with the stature of the bottle, which holds 4.5 litres, the production staff painted a giant letter 'I' in black on a white sheet and hung it over the 'E' on the 'ARDBEG' sign on the whitewashed wall of the distillery which faces out to sea. Thus, 'ARDBEG' became 'ARDBIG' for the day.

During the same Festival, visitors paid £1 for the privilege of writing personal messages on slates which were subsequently used during the reconstruction of Ardbeg's third pagoda, which had been destroyed in a storm the previous January. The money was donated to a local charity, and as Glenmorangie notes "These slates were gathered by our warehousemen and the roofers proceeded to lay them on to the new pagoda. Our visitors and committee members have now become part of the fabric of the building. Thanks!"

Previous Festival ploys have included creating the 'People's Republic of South Islay,' featuring the theme of a military coup. Staff members rushed to dress up in black berets, combat fatigues and dark glasses, Che Guevara style. The theme of the event focused on being shot against a wall, though happily for visitors, the shooting was done with a camera, and their 'mugshots' were subsequently displayed in the visitor centre. "They even re-created the 'Bay of Pigs' down at the beach," recalls Hamish Torrie, "comprising a black sow and piglets that Jackie got hold of!"

'Brand loyalty' to Ardbeg sometimes starts at a very early age, as Stuart Thomson explains:

"When our sons Robbie and Harry were five and two respectively, we took them down to Cornwall on holiday. They're very different characters. Robbie is quiet, while Harry is just the opposite. It was a beautiful day, two o'clock on a Saturday afternoon. As we looked for somewhere to eat we found this wonderful restaurant. We were dressed very casually, with the sort of ridiculous shorts you wear on holiday, but the clientele of the restaurant was not like this, they were wearing jackets and bow ties and lovely dresses, and drinking Champagne. When we walked in, they all looked up at us as if we shouldn't be there. We wondered about the

wisdom of eating there with Harry, but then we found some seats outside, so we stayed. The food was delightful, and Harry fed the small, cherry tomatoes to the ducks and geese.

"When we walked in to pay you could hear the cutlery going down and feel everyone looking at us again. We went up to the bar to pay and we noticed they had this wonderful selection of whiskies. All of a sudden Harry points to an optic and says 'Phroaig!' Sure enough, it was Laphroaig, and don't forget, he was only two years old. Then he points to another bottle and says 'Vulin, Vulin' and, sure enough, it was Lagavulin. I thought it was fantastic that he had noticed two Islay malts and all these posh people were taking notice.

Now by this time, Jackie had stopped being uncomfortable and was acting the proud mum, and everyone in the restaurant was watching and listening. 'But there's no Ardbeg,' said Jackie. At which point Harry said loudly, 'Oh ****'. You could have heard a pin drop. We left very rapidly, and back at the car I was asked the inevitable question by Jackie. 'Did you teach him to swear?'

'No I didn't,' I replied. 'It must have been some of the guys at the distillery!'"

Despite Stuart's close bond with his workforce and the passion he has for Ardbeg, the time came for him to seek new challenges, and the distillery and brand he did so much to shape are clearly in good health for the future. At the time of his departure from Ardbeg, Stuart Thomson wrote to the Committee members in August 2006:

Dear Committee Members and friends,

As your Chairman for the last five and a half years I have thoroughly enjoyed watching our beloved Ardbeg grow from a whisky known by a few to a malt increasingly recognised across the world.

Who would have believed this could have happened when I arrived in 1997 with the backing of The Glenmorangie Company to breathe new life into a Distillery that by all measures was nearly lost forever. The transformation in those 9 years has been quite extraordinary, extremely exciting and yes, from time to time a little scary... especially when the roof of the Old Kiln blew off in the hurricane of January 1999!

The passion and enthusiasm you have shown for Ardbeg and indeed the support you have given me and the team at the Distillery has been one of the most rewarding parts of my job. Many of you have made the arduous journey to Islay to wonder along with myself at the remarkable renaissance of this proud Distillery.

In no small measure this is down to you, the Committee, who have spread the word about Ardbeg and its indomitable spirit to the four corners of the globe to the extent that the Committee now numbers some 35,000 members in 112 countries!

So it is with great regret that this note announces my departure from Ardbeg. I have been considering this for some time not because of any dimming of my passion for The Ultimate Islay Malt - more because there comes a time in life when it's quite simply time for a change.

I shall be leaving Ardbeg soon to go off to pastures new, but one thing I will always carry with me are memories of all the conversations, e-mails, tastings, discussions, debates and comradeship we have had over the years. My admiration for Ardbeg under Glenmorangie's stewardship remains as strong as ever.

I wish my successor well and go off to my next adventure bolstered with pride in all that I and the team at the Distillery and Old Kiln have achieved together. I, of course, remain a member of the Committee and look forward to keeping in touch.

Slainte

Stuart Thomson

Keen-eyed Harry Thomson

The Ark Royal anchored
just off Ardbeg (opposite)

Mor Ardbeg

Mary and her team work particularly hard in the kitchen during the Festival making Ardbeg Burgers, among other delights

Eddie Brown and his band, including his daughter Rebecca,
provide some local entertainment to keep spirits high

Emma McGechie and Jackie Thompson

SAMPLING THE SPIRIT

CHAPTER EIGHT

Highly valued by blenders, historically Ardbeg has enjoyed a modest but persistent level of support as a single malt, with a steady flow of requests to the distillery for it. Initially these requests were for small, 'octave' casks, and latterly for bottles. However, due to the strong demand for Ardbeg as a blending whisky, it was never considered necessary or viable to actively market it as a single malt. Consequently, until recent times, the Ardbeg 'brand' has had virtually nothing spent on it in marketing terms, and very little spirit was ever bottled as a malt, resulting in it developing a 'cult' status.

Back in 1921 the idea of introducing a blend "purely made from not more than 25% old grain such as Cambus and 75% Ardbeg about 5yo" was considered. According to Colin E Hay, the distillery manager, "There is no doubt that in the colonies it is blended whisky they look for and their taste for a single pure malt whisky has not had a chance of being cultivated."

Hamish Scott, distillery manager from 1964, says "We filled one cask in 1964 for putting down. It was in poor wood, and the whisky tasted very woody back then. We eventually started filling into decent wood in the '70s."

Having sampled some of the very first distillery bottlings, released in the 1970s, it is surprising to note the comparative lightness and 'approachability' of these expressions, both on the nose and palate. Having gained a reputation as the most heavily-peated single malt whisky in the world, and with the malt used in these bottlings being produced on the distillery floor maltings, there was an expectation of a much more challenging whisky.

Interestingly, we evaluated one of the earliest official Ardbeg bottlings side by side with a 10-year-old Cadenhead bottling, comprising spirit distilled and bottled in the same year, courtesy of Han Van Wees (see panel). Unlike the distillery offerings, the Cadenhead bottling epitomised the anticipated character of 'old' Ardbeg. It was a robust, salty, peaty, commanding Ardbeg, which offers characteristics far from evident in subsequent distillery bottlings. Former Allied Distillers' blender Robert Hicks described Ardbeg from the 1970s as being "like tarry rope or creosote," and the Cadenhead bottling most accurately reflects those descriptors.

"You must try old Ardbeg if you can, the old ten-year-old bottlings," insists Sukhinder Singh of The Whisky Exchange (see Chapter 9). "It's got a balance, complexity and flavour you'll fall in love with. The peat is so sober and subtle after all the lovely fruit flavours have come and gone. The peat is right at the back, whereas with the recent Ardbegs you get the peat at the front."

Overall, both distillery and independent bottlings of Ardbeg display wide variations of style. Despite this, the whisky has been considered one of the most highly prized of all single malts by most, if not all, experts. According to the late Michael Jackson ... "Every connoisseur regards Ardbeg as one of the greats…"

Whisky writer Jim Murray has long been one of Ardbeg's most vociferous champions, declaring it to be "Unquestionably the greatest distillery to be found on earth," and in his 2008 *Whisky Bible* he awarded Ardbeg 10-year-old the supreme accolade of 'World Whisky of the Year.'

Current Ardbeg distillery manager Mickey Heads says "I've always liked the spirit itself. It's got lightness and fruit and floral notes, then smoke. Then a big explosion in the mouth. There's a lot going on in the spirit. People are looking for flavour in their whisky, not just knocking it back any more. They now nose and taste their whiskies and know what they're doing. They want flavour."

Jackie Thomson declares "Ardbeg has a wonderful, complex aroma, and the peat doesn't wallop you in the face. There's lots of complexity on the nose to entice you in. There's an incongruity in the huge phenol content but with lots of sweetness. We have the highest regular phenol content in the industry. Hidden depths.

"We sometimes get bottles back from consumers saying that it tastes of cleaning fluid! They'll say things like 'I bought it for my husband as a present, and it's not that he's not a malt drinker, because we've got a bottle of Glenfiddich in the cupboard.' Often the bottles are almost empty! I try to phone them and talk to them. I think it's important we deal with complaints like that and try to explain to people what Ardbeg is about."

Sukhinder Singh echoes Jackie's points about complexity and peatiness. "I like Ardbeg's complexity," he says. "Although supposedly the peatiest of the Islays, it doesn't appear that peaty to me because it's so well balanced. That's pretty amazing. The balance and complexity are very important to me in whiskies.

"I also like fruitiness in whisky, and the nice thing about drinking young whiskies is you get the fruit coming through. I want to get fruit flavours and nuts. Some of the best Ardbegs I've tried were very young ones. I like Almost There particularly, but not the previous two young bottlings. A little too immature for me. I think the concept and the pricing were good, but they were not really my style of whisky."

"Believe it or not," says Glenmorangie's Bill Lumsden, "I had only tasted Ardbeg once before we bought the distillery! When Jim Murray came to see me at Glenmorangie, he always used to go on about Ardbeg, but I was probably a bit dismissive, thinking it was not really my style of whisky. Jim introduced me to it at the Machrie Hotel on Islay, just after we bought the distillery, and I was absolutely blown away. It was a Gordon & MacPhail Connoisseur's Choice 1978 vintage and I was hooked after that."

Reflecting the wide stylistic diversity apparent within Ardbeg bottlings, Bill notes that "There was a huge variation in the cask styles we bought with the distillery. Each year's distillation seems to be different: 1978 was very elegant and fruity, '77 was my favourite, with a beautiful fudged, toffee character to it, '75 was oily, diesely, gutsy, really full on. A lot of refill casks had been used.

"Even I find the full on, gutsy 1975 challenging, but the '77 was the 'bee's knees.' 1977 undoubtedly had the classic Ardbeg notes of tarry rope, like Band Aid, a bit of sherbet lime in the background, but a lovely, round, fudgy note to it which smoothed the whole lot out. It was a very complete whisky. '78 also had lots of classic Ardbeg notes, but it was fruitier, with Florida Key lime pie sensation!"

Former manager Stuart Thomson recalls "Iain Henderson loved Ardbeg; he knew how good it was. He came up a month after we started production and I gave him a taste of the new make. He turned round and said 'That is absolutely beautiful.'"

Han Van Wees feels that the current Ardbeg is sweeter, preferring the drier style of whisky produced during the 1960s and early '70s.

Below is a selection of tasting notes, including some provided by Bill Lumsden, complemented by views from Belgian Ardbeg collector Geert Bero (see Chapter 9) and Sukhinder Singh.

RELEASES PRIOR TO GLENMORANGIE OWNERSHIP

Prior to the 1970s, little attention was paid to cask selection, resulting in the spirit being stored in casks of varying quality, often imparting little influence to the maturing whisky. Consequently, much of the whisky that was bottled by the distillery in the 1970s and '80s was relatively dry, light and fruity. With the additional fluctuations associated with floor maltings, there was a relatively wide variation in the style of spirit being produced.

HAN VAN WEES

Along with his son, Maurice, Han Van Wees operates the Van Wees company from a shop on the outskirts of the Dutch city of Amersfoort, where some 1,200 whiskies are on sale. The origins of the family firm date back to 1921, when Han's father established a wholesale tobacco business, and from 1963 onwards Van Wees developed a secondary role distributing and retailing spirits. Since 1975 the concentration has been solely on spirits, with Van Wees acting as a whisky wholesaler to shops throughout Europe, and also bottling single casks under the 'Ultimate Single Malt Scotch Whisky Selection' label.

"Our clients started to ask us for malt whisky," recalls Han, "but you couldn't even buy it in London. So we began to specialise in importing malt whisky, and once we started doing this, customers from France and Germany as well as Holland came to buy malt from us. We were the first to import single malt Scotch whisky into mainland western Europe.

"In 1965 we bought casks of Ardbeg, Bowmore and Laphroaig from the Dutch Distillers company. They had been blending these with their own spirit, but by this time the market for the Dutch whisky they made was over – it was too expensive compared to blended Scotch. At that time you couldn't buy malt whisky from the Scottish distilleries, so this was how we got hold of some. We bought a hogshead of Ardbeg initially, and bottled it.

"Dutch Distillers only had Islays because they needed something with character to blend with their own spirit. Our bottling of the Islay malts was a great success. Subsequently, we imported virtually all the Scotch malt whiskies, except Glenfiddich and Balvenie, into Hollland.

"In 1976 we bought 50 cases of Ardbeg, and it sold so well that less than a year later we tried to get another 50 cases. We were told that the distillery didn't have any stock and we would have to wait until they got more orders, so we asked Cadenhead in Aberdeen to bottle two casks of Ardbeg for us instead. Two days later the distillery told us they now had orders from Japan and elsewhere so they were able to go ahead and bottle our 50 cases. We ended up with 50 cases of each!

"The two batches turned up within a week of each other, and I preferred the Cadenhead to the distillery bottling. We sold the distillery bottling and then the Cadenhead, and today I just have one open bottle of each left!

"We also bought lots of Connoisseur's Choice Ardbeg from Gordon & MacPhail in Elgin, and they bottled between 10 and 20 casks for us under their 'Spirit of Scotland' label. In my opinion, the 1993 Connoisseur's Choice bottling of Ardbeg, bottled in 2005, is one of the best of all time. It is drier than many bottlings, and has the typical smells and tastes that I associated with Ardbeg."

In 1973 Ardbeg first began to supplement its own malt production with an external supply, which means that spirit distilled in 1972 is the last totally Ardbeg-peated whisky. Initially 10 per cent, and then 15 per cent, of externally-malted barley was used, and this is unlikely to have affected the overall character of Ardbeg until 1977 when Hiram Walker experimented with considerably higher levels of externally- produced malt, even up to 100 per cent.

By 1975 bottling Ardbeg as a single malt was being considered more seriously by the company Board. Following a bottling in July of that year "Mr Scott reported that the initial reaction to the Ardbeg bottled in July had been encouraging, but it was very difficult to asses what future demand might be. The board agreed to continue bottling Ardbeg on a small scale." Hamish Scott wrote in a letter dated 19th June 1975 "Our whisky is a very traditional Islay malt having a distinctive peaty bouquet, although not as heavy as some others."

Pre-Hiram Walker bottling with white label and illustration of distillery

"Very clean and sharp, with a slight smell of burnt plastic – but in a good way. A cow byre. Very dirty, but oh so drinkable! For me, this is a fantastic whisky. The ten-year-old is much better than the 12-year-old. You don't need to add water, drink it neat. It's already at 40%ABV." *Geert Bero*

Hiram Walker 10-year-old bottling in clear glass with black label, white and gold text (Released 1977/78, whisky from early 1960s)

"I call it whisky for playing cards. You sit down with a group of friends to play cards, and by the end of the evening the bottle is empty. It's quite light and gently peated – highly drinkable." *Geert Bero*

Hiram Walker 10-year-old bottling in green glass with black labels, white and gold text (Released c.1983)

"Mediocre whisky. Disappointing, I really thought it would be better." *Geert Bero*

Allied 15-year-old bottling in green glass with black labels, white and gold text

"This was sold in a package with an accompanying bottle of Laphroaig, and it's even worse than the ten-year-old!" *Geert Bero*

Allied 30-year-old bottling in green glass with black labels, white and gold text (Released 1996/7, comprising whisky from the 1960s)

"Dark oloroso Sherry wood. Very much a dessert whisky, ideal with pancakes. A very good whisky." *Geert Bero*

GENERAL RELEASES UNDER GLENMORANGIE OWNERSHIP

Ardbeg Provenance (first released 1997)
55.6% ABV
"A very great whisky. The Asia bottling of 2000 at 55%ABV is the best. The Provenance from 1974 is a vatting of casks which has some amazing whiskies in it." *Geert Bero*

Ardbeg Ten Years Old (first released 2000)
46.0% ABV
Exceptional balance and depth on the nose. At full strength, the aroma is a seductive mix of toffee and chocolate sweetness, cinnamon spice and medicinal phenols. Fresh citrus notes of white wine are evident as are melon, pear drops, general creaminess, fresh phenolic aroma of seaspray (iodine) and smoked fish. Hickory and coffee emerge later as the most volatile top notes fade. On the palate, an initial moderate and clean sweetness is rapidly followed by a mouthful of

deep peat notes, with tobacco smoke and strong espresso coffee, which then gives way to treacle sweetness and liquorice. The mouth-feel is firstly lightly spiced (astringent), then chewing, mouth-watering, full and finally dry. The finish is long and smoky. A smoky sweetness is left on the palate, with a crushed peat and sweet malted cereal character.
(Tasting notes courtesy Dr Bill Lumsden)

Ardbeg Lord of the Isles (first released 2001) 46.0%ABV
An exceptionally deep, rich and sweet nose: the sweetness of chocolate, marzipan and cherries, surrounding a deep and peaty centre. Cocoa and a rich maltiness are discovered with layers of smoke and salt, giving wood smoke and saddle soap. Later, there is a hint of mandarin fruit and a gentle heather and lavender scent. The taste is initially sweet with vanilla and chocolate giving way rapidly to a crescendo of peat and cocoa. The finish is long and dry with chocolate malt, cocoa and crushed peat resting satisfyingly on the palate.
(Tasting notes courtesy Dr Bill Lumsden)

"A fantastic whisky with beautiful fruit in the middle." *Sukhinder Singh*

"For price and quality it's one of the best Ardbeg's on the market. The first batch, from 2001, is the best. A lot of Sherry influence and a really nice, drinkable whisky. You can easily drink several glasses of it. It has a kind of lightness. If you drank a Lord of the Isles then a Macallan you would still be able to taste the Macallan properly. That's a mark of how drinkable Lord of the Isles is. The earlier batches were heavier – maybe some Kildalton spirit went into the later ones to make it lighter" *Geert Bero*

Ardbeg Uigeadail (first released 2003) 54.2% ABV
The undiluted nose is deep and rounded – chocolate caramels and barley sugar combine with dates, raisins and smooth Sherry notes. Later, you find leather and linseed oil. With water the sweetness gives way to malted honeycomb, with flowering currants emerging through the smoky sweetness of a well-fired fruit pudding. On the palate, sweet, chewy and oily with a silky mouth-feel. The flavour is initially sweet, revealing fruit cake and treacle. This is followed by smoked barbecue or honey-roast food with the slightest hint of olives. The finish is long, both sweet and dry with honey, treacle and a trace of mint.
(Tasting notes courtesy Dr Bill Lumsden)

"It has changed quite a lot from bottling to bottling. The 2003 is the best, but then the first batch of anything released is almost always the best. I like the Sherry influence in this expression, I think it works very well, and I like the aspect of mystique in the Gaelic names given to this and to bottlings like Airigh nam Beist." *Geert Bero*

Ardbeg Kildalton (released 2004) 57.6% ABV
"Our limited edition 1980 Kildalton bottling was not completely unpeated," stresses Bill Lumsden, "but was peated to just 4-5ppm. We produced 1,300 bottles and they sold like hot cakes. We offered it at Christmas 2004. It had amazing delicacy, fruity and floral esters and aldehydes came through, along with a waxiness from the wooden washbacks. We released it to give a glimpse of the delicacy you get in 'new make' Ardbeg. Brand Director Hamish Torrie makes the interesting point that "Ardbeg new spirit has the same amount of esters, aldehydes and all these fruity floral character that Glenmorangie has, but you do not usually find them because they are woven in or hidden by the phenols. Unpeated Ardbeg gives an indication of the delicacy within Ardbeg. Waxiness from the pine washbacks adds balance to the heavy phenols."

Ardbeg 1965 (released 2005)
42.1 %ABV
Initial wafts of sea spray on the nose give way to a mix of luscious summer fruits (blackberries and blueberries) enveloped in ripe peaches. Beneath the mouth-watering fruit, nutty chocolate and vanilla notes emerge. The senses are latterly aware of sweet smokiness, coal tar and gentle peat oils. With water the sweet smokiness becomes more apparent; subtle medicinal, tarry rope notes are suggested with briny sea spray as the senses are reminded of its Islay birthplace. The theme is still fruity and fragrant, with top notes of wine gums and autumn brambles. The flavours open further, revealing waxy aromatics, chocolate raisins and rich fruitcake. Subdued traces of tree sap and tobacco smoke are present in the background. The mouth-feel is warming with a tingly effect. The flavour is initially of a salty sea breeze with fish smoked over an open heather and peat fire. In a few seconds, rich dried fruits (raisins and sultanas) come to the fore with elements of cherry pie and ice cream. Vanilla is present throughout, with peat, espresso coffee and berry fruits completing a myriad of flavours. The long finish lingers with peat smoke and blackcurrants, with hints of dark chocolate, dried fruit and traces of sea salt.
(Tasting notes courtesy Dr Bill Lumsden)

"Disappointing. I get quite a strong rum flavour from it – almost as though it has been in a rum cask at some point?" *Geert Bero*

Ardbeg Airigh Nam Beist (first released 2006)
46.0%ABV
Smoky, ice cream, fennel, pine nuts and zesty limes on the nose. Peppery, oily mouth-feel. Maple syrup, smoky bacon, antiseptic lozenges, some vanilla, smoked meats and barbecue spices on the palate. The finish is zesty, smoky and intriguing.
(Tasting notes courtesy Dr Bill Lumsden)
"A round, full whisky, well matured. The 2006 rotation in particular is very good" *Geert Bero*

"Like Uigeadail, the 1990 Airigh nan Beist is a fantastic, beautiful whisky. They illustrate the great variety of styles that can comprise Ardbeg." *Sukhinder Singh*

Ardbeg Mor (released 2007)
57.3%ABV
"A big whisky in every sense. It's a good whisky, and if you compare it to the Very Young you see how important maturation is to whisky" *Geert Bero*

Vintages
1975 (bottled in 1989/99/2000/2001)
"all fantastic whiskies." *Geert Bero*

1977 (bottled in 2001 and 2004)
"Very peaty, yet clean and sharp as a knife." *Geert Bero*

1990 (bottled in 2004)
"Not the best 1990, but I still like it. I think the best 1990 is Airigh nam Beist." *Geert Bero*

SINGLE CASKS RELEASES UNDER GLENMORANGIE OWNERSHIP

Inevitably, Glenmorangie inherited a significant amount of 1974 spirit, as over one million litres was produced that year, just before the Ardbeg business faced a dramatic downturn. Consequently, most of the single cask releases have been of spirit produced in 1974, reflecting one of the distillery's finest years with numerous exceptional casks.

Favourite single cask bottlings of Geert Bero include "Cask 2782 from 1972, Cask 2781, bottled for the French market and Cask 2780, done for the Danish market. These were from ex-Bourbon casks and were clearer and sharper than my overall favourite Cask 2391, different but also very good. The Islay Festival bottling for 2002, Cask 2390 also comprises the dark Sherry and peated whisky combination. I think it's sad that none of the Islay distilleries fill a lot of Sherry casks anymore. There are a lot of good single cask releases out there, and just two bad ones I know about. One for the Swedish market and one for hotel bars."

Cask 2391 Manager's Choice (Released 1999)
56%ABV

"My personal favourite is the Manager's Choice Cask 2391 bottling from 1976. Oloroso Sherry together with peated whisky, it's a really good marriage. The dark Sherry style works really well with Ardbeg. It's got everything – complexity, sweet aromas of the Sherry and lovely peat. A cracking choice by Stuart, his first Single Cask Manager's Choice, and it certainly proved he has a real nose for it!" *Geert Bero*

Casks 2392 & 2394 (Released 2000)
55% & 53.2%ABV

Released exclusively for the Committee (see chapter 6 for the story behind this release)
"Simply a beautiful, beautiful whisky " *Stuart Thomson*

"Two of my favourites" *Geert Bero*

Cask 1375 (Released 2006)
54.2%ABV (1975)

This single cask combines raisin chocolate, cherry cakes and Garibaldi biscuits. Citrus notes of lemon rind mingle with gentle wood smoke and elderflower in the aroma, while sweet toffee apples, spicy nutmeg, delicious lemon cake and ripe blackberries tantalise the tastebuds. The finish is spicy and smoky with the sweetness of lime and a touch of black pepper.
(Tasting notes courtesy Dr Bill Lumsden)

WHISKY PRODUCED UNDER GLENMORANGIE OWNERSHIP

Ardbeg Very Young (released 2004)
58.3%ABV

Sweet toffee, chocolate, hints of treacle and Butterkist popcorn on the nose. Something gently smoky lurking in the background. The delicious, treacly, charcoal smoke reveals itself fully on the palate, with hints of herbs and malt. The finish offers a long treacle and cloves aftertaste.
(Tasting notes courtesy Dr Bill Lumsden)

"Disappointed! I know a lot of people have been unhappy with this, it is too young" *Geert Bero*

Ardbeg Still Young (released 2006)
56.2%ABV

We couldn't possibly have conceived at the time just how enthusiastically folk would embrace the idea of Very Young Ardbeg. Indeed, many enthusiasts are keen to continue to sample our work in progress. So its spirited sibling, Still Young, followed it along the peaty path to full maturity. Still youthful and zesty but definitely more creamy and rounded from extra ageing, this character is a wonderful addition to the family.
(Tasting notes courtesy Dr Bill Lumsden)

"Getting better, but still too young!" *Geert Bero*

Ardbeg Almost There (released 2007)
54.1%ABV

An intriguing nose of peat bogs, pine cones and birch tar, interlaced with the sweetness of fudge and caramel toffees and just a tang of salt.
(Tasting notes courtesy Dr Bill Lumsden)

"It's getting there – you can really feel the extra maturation of the extra three years. For me, the names sum them up. Very Young is just that, and so is Still Young" *Geert Bero*

As Ardbeg's Jackie Thomson notes, "Very Young had a really phenolic nose, and Still Young was much creamier and a bit woodier. People expected Almost There to keep the creaminess, but it's surprised them. It's more phenolic than you might expect, rather back to the style of the Very Young. We're not sure which way it will go for the ten-year-old. The jury's out, and it's quite exciting."

THE WHISKY-MAKERS ON WHISKY

Malcolm Rennie

I didn't start to drink whisky until I went to Ardbeg to work. I'd not really had many peaty whiskies because I'd been working at Bunnahabhain and Bruichladdich, and the peatiness just won me over.

Mackie - Ruaraidh Macintyre

I like to drink the Bailie Nicol Jarvie blend with Drambuie and Crabbie's Green Ginger added to it. If I know I'm going to be out for a long night I'll drink vodka.

Asha – Alistair Johnston

If I'm having a drink in the house on a Saturday night it's usually red wine, but I do enjoy a dram of Ardbeg. The 17-year-old is the best to my mind. Everybody in the distillery will tell you it's the best. They do fancy bottlings of the really good stuff, maybe just 200 or 300 bottles, and it probably never gets drunk. Whisky is made to drink!

Azza – Alec Livingstone

I'd say Ardbeg was definitely a man's dram. Most of the boys here like Glen Moray as well, and I like it as a contrast sometimes. I enjoy Ardbeg 17-year-old and Uigeadail most. Back in the 1960s and '70s there were a few wobbly men around the place, what with the legal drams they were given during their shifts and a few others you could scooch up here and there.

Drew – Andrew Mullen

I used to drink Teacher's and Bell's and then moved on to Jack Daniel's. Then I met Tracy, my partner, and she introduced me to Black Bottle as the local blend on Islay. Now I'm spoilt rotten!

Alistair Blair

What you're making today won't be used for another 10 years. I'm looking forward to seeing a bottle I was involved in making in 10 years' time, and that's quite a personal investment. I've been known to drink the old 17-year-old. It was the very first malt whisky I ever tasted. My father had drunk it for years. I didn't even know where Ardbeg was – but he's very proud of me now!

Wardie

One day we were 'tapping' the casks with a rod to check for any that didn't sound full and might have been leaking in warehouse 5 when we just took a half bottle out of a quarter cask. I remember it was owned by Stewart's of Dundee. We didn't drink much at that time, so nobody was tailing us! The old cooper used to top up casks with 'new make' if they seemed to be going down a bit quick. It wasn't allowed by law, of course.

I like the 17-year-old Ardbeg myself, and the Airigh nam Beist. I have bottles of the old ten-year-old and other rare ones being kept by members of my family all over the island so I'm not tempted to drink them!

"TARRY ROPE"

Sampling the various expressions of Ardbeg that have been bottled over the years provides a marvellous insight into just how much a whisky from one distillery can vary in character. The vast majority of Ardbeg bottlings range from 'great' to 'stunning' and yet they are so different. Generally, all have the peat, smoke and fruit with floral and briny notes most readily associated with Ardbeg, but these attributes are discerned to varying degrees and are sometimes most evident on the nose in one expression while being more evident in the taste or finish in another.

While the owners of Ardbeg in the 1980s and '90s were not interested in marketing Ardbeg as a single malt, many excellent casks left the distillery and were stowed away by independent bottlers, offering an even wider exposure to aspects of Ardbeg's character.

Bert Vuik of Holland has a particularly fine collection of independent Ardbeg bottlings from pre-1981, when the distillery closed for eight years and the in-house floor maltings were shut down forever. Interestingly, some of these independent bottlings are highly prized by collectors and enthusiasts, with a Cadenhead brown, dumpy-shaped bottle, distilled in 1959, selling for well over £1,000. According to Bert, "Mostly these bottlings are valuable to me personally not in money terms. As far as prices of Ardbeg are concerned, the sums of money that are paid for some Ardbegs are totally crazy, at least to my mind."

Many of Bert's bottles are open and he kindly provided us with ten samples which display the considerable range of styles offered by Ardbeg. As former Allied master blender Robert Hicks sums up Ardbeg's character as "tarry rope", we set out to discover which expressions best resembled that 'house' style.

Tasted by Graeme Wallace, the expressions are listed in order of personal preference, with the ultimate expression, and indeed the one with the strongest tarry rope attributes, being listed last.

Kingsbury: Ardbeg distilled 1967, bottled 1996 as 29-year-old at 54.6%. Cask 922

Not being a big Sherrywood fan, I find this expression is simply overpowered by Sherry.

Cadenhead: Ardbeg distilled 1965 as 24-year-old at 54.4% 75cl Dumpy, brown bottle.

A light and pleasant, sweet damp and briny nose, with a nice dry and tarry palate, although a bit wanting. A long-lasting pear finish, but a little bitter.

Samaroli: Ardbeg distilled 1973, bottled 1988 at 57%. Fragments of Scotland. A promising, strong, sweet and briny start to the nose. Spicy and soft, slightly sweet and rather salty on the palate, with a soft, briny finish.

Signatory: Ardbeg distilled 1967, bottled 1997 at 52%. Cask 578, one of 540 bottles.

Although still dark in colour, the Sherry is more subdued in this expression than in the Kingsbury, but is still clearly evident. A sweet Sherry palate which masks the peat. Eventually, the peat becomes more evident at the end, despite the very pleasant and long lingering Sherry notes.

Cadenhead: Ardbeg 17-year-old at 46% 75cl. Dumpy, brown bottle.

Archetypal Ardbeg nose – sweet peat, slightly tarry, fragrant and inviting. The palate is lighter that the nose suggests, with a strong wave of peat coming through at the end. A long woody, briny finish. Very nice, but still not the best Cadenhead bottling we have tasted

Douglas Laing: Ardbeg distilled 1973, bottled 2003 at 51.9%. Platinum. One of 94 bottles.

Damp sawdust first comes to the fore, followed by sweet pears. The palate is sweet and very fruity, although it lacks much peat. A smokiness develops right at the end, then just lingers on and on!

The next three expressions offer quite differing characteristics. They are all excellent and deserve equal credit:

Cadenhead: Ardbeg distilled 1974, bottled 1992 at 54.9% Authentic Collection.

Rich, sweet wood, with briny and fishy attributes, introduce this expression. The palate is dominated by salt, although there is also a clear, briny, smoky taste clawing the inside of your mouth. The salt-sweet cocktail lingers and lingers.

Kingsbury: Ardbeg distilled 1974, bottled 2000 at 50%. One of 278 bottles.

Wet sawdust and sweet peat please the nose, while a creamy fruitiness dominates the palate. A salty, smooth finish goes up in a puff of smoke at the end. Great balance. So different to the previous expression yet equally pleasing and distilled in the same year!

Samaroli: Ardbeg distilled 1974, bottled 1983 at 59%. Sherry wood. One of 2,400 bottles.

Strong, burnt wood dominates the nose like a warming bonfire. A richness caries through to the palate; clean, sweet, fruity and delicious. A sweet spicy and delicate finish. Full and rich, here the Sherry has supported the maturation rather than dominated it.

Dun Eideann: Ardbeg distilled 1972, bottled 1991 at 58.9%. Cask 3444. One of 320 bottles.

A very rich and thick treacle sweetness together with damp sawdust is clearly evident to the nose. On the palate, this becomes a real powerhouse of flavours. It is thick, clawing and has everything in huge quantities – lots of peat, briny yet sweet, lovely fruit and, yes, tarry rope! The finish is equally satisfying – sweet, tarry, briny and oh so long.

COLLECTING ARDBEG

CHAPTER NINE

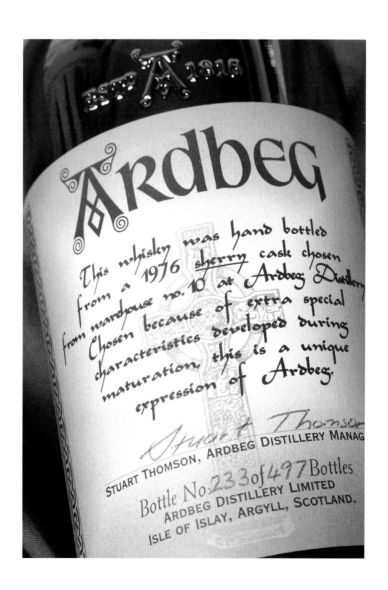

Single malt Scotch whisky has become increasingly collectible during the past two decades, and no brand is more desirable than Ardbeg, with values growing significantly in the last two to three years.

With a burgeoning cult status and very few bottlings released prior to Glenmorangie's acquisition of the distillery in 1997, there is relatively little 'old' Ardbeg to collect, making every limited release under Glenmorangie instantly attractive to aficionados.

A number of expressions released in the last decade have more than quadrupled in price, while, somewhat surprisingly, some the original distillery bottlings from the 1970s remain relatively affordable. Indeed, some of the more recent bottlings, such as Provenance and a few of the single cask releases, have attained particularly high values in excess of £1,000.

One of the world's leading Ardbeg collectors is Geert Bero, co-owner and manager of the Hotel Bero in Ostend, Belgium. The hotel was established by his great-grandfather in 1921 as "a pub with just three bedrooms above it." Not only does Geert's collection encompass virtually every distillery bottling of Ardbeg ever released, including each label variant and market-specific bottling, but he also has many duplicates.

Geert usually has in excess of 100 open bottles, many of which may be sampled in the Hotel Bero's 'On the Rocks' whisky bar, which now boasts some 90 whiskies. They are also used for sampling sessions, and, of course, for simply enjoying with friends in his Ardbeg-themed studio apartment. Among his many whisky-related activities, Geert is a member of the exclusive Lindores Whisky Society, which has its clubroom base at the Hotel Bero. It comprises 11 friends from all over Belgium who visit festivals and Scotch whisky distilleries several times a year. The Society even hosts its own annual festival at the Hotel Bero.

"Ardbeg has been made what it is by the people out there who drink it," insists Geert. "I think Ardbeg made its name because of the old bottlings, which connoisseurs have bought and opened." His personal interest in Scotch whisky began in 1998, when "I drank some 14-year-old Oban, and that got me hooked on single malts. In 2002 I was at a tasting in our hotel which had an Ardbeg single cask bottling in it and that was so good I said I had to have more, although I already had bottles of the 10 and 17-year-olds.

"Back in 2002 Ardbeg was just beginning to become popular, but you could still afford to buy the older bottlings. The most I've paid for a bottle is Euros 1,900. That was a rare clear bottle with a black label and white letters. My advice to anyone contemplating starting to collect Ardbeg now is simple. Think twice, as prices have already risen a great deal, and there's going to be a lot of money involved."

Geert aims to have at least one example of every official bottling in his collection, no matter how minor the variations. As he explains, "Even a small change in a back label is significant. But this is Utopia, because I don't know if I'll ever find some of the oldest bottlings. The hunt is sometimes more fun than the final discovery of what you've been looking for."

He makes the significant point that "I'm a whisky drinker as well as a collector. I always have a lot of bottles open. It's sad when people collect whisky and don't know what it's like."

Along with fellow Scotch whisky devotees, Geert makes regular pilgrimages to Scotland to visit distilleries and purchase whisky, and sometimes the purchasing can get a little out of hand, as he recalls of one trip undertaken in 2004. "That time we had three people in the car and 140 bottles on the way home! The customs officer at Rosyth in Fife where we were catching the ferry back to Belgium looked at all the bottles and just said 'Okay, drive on.' He didn't mind – we'd just been supporting the Scottish economy."

Collecting any commodity can become an obsession, but as someone whose bottles are frequently opened and consumed too, Geert is always on the lookout for sources of well-priced Ardbeg. "One day in 2003 I got an email from the guy at World of Whiskies at Heathrow Airport," he says. "He told me they had bottles of Ardbeg Provenance at £225 per bottle. In Belgium it was already selling for the equivalent of £700 per bottle. So I flew from Brussels to Heathrow and never left terminal four. I just bought seven bottles of it and waited for the next flight back. That's how crazy you can be for a bottle of whisky!"

As that anecdote illustrates, having established a reputation as one of the leading collectors of Ardbeg, Geert is often approached by individuals and retailers offering to sell him bottles of Ardbeg, and these offers are rarely turned down. One of the principal sources of Geert's collection has been the London-based The Whisky Exchange, owned by Sukhinder Singh.

The Whisky Exchange is principally an online whisky retailing operation, which has now been trading for a decade. The Exchange not only retails an impressively large range of single malts, but uniquely also sells old, collectible and rare bottlings. In addition to this, Sukhinder is himself a serious collector, favouring in particular Port Ellen and Ardbeg single malts.

"I actually started as a collector in 1987," he notes, "and I'm still a collector first and foremost. I grew up in the industry really, as my parents had shops and the family collected miniature bottles. I really got into that, I was intrigued by them and at one point I purchased a collection of 8,000 miniatures. That was really too many. I was a member of the Mini Bottle Club and I found that 90 per cent of their members collected whisky, so I decided to do the same, but that still left 4,000 bottles! I then decided to specialise in single malts, which cut it down to around 400."

After studying chartered surveying at university, Sukhinder joined the family business, and progressed to collecting full-size bottles. "It was just one from each distillery, and only old bottlings to begin with," he says. "I was happy to spend lots of money on just one or two bottles a year, but then around 1993 came the start of the whisky collecting boom, with Black Bowmore, limited edition Glenmorangie and so on.

"I felt then that with so much happening I couldn't limit myself to just one bottle from each distillery, so being in the trade, I was able to order cases of new whiskies, and sell bottles on to friends, keeping some for myself. The first bottle I opened to drink was a 21-year-old Springbank. I wasn't a whisky drinker until then. The second was the old Ardbeg 10-year-old and after that it was a case of 'what do I try next?' It was a trail of discovery."

Ten years ago Sukhinder's parents retired, selling their retail business, and as Sukhinder recalls, "At that point my brother and I decided to retail whisky. The first year was very hard, buying and selling to maybe 20 to 30 friends – some of the most serious and knowledgeable whisky people I still know. They got me off the ground." He stresses that "Ardbeg is very important to me as a collector and a drinker."

Like Geert Bero, Sukhinder is not averse to opening bottles, and makes the important observation that "Whisky can never become collectible unless it's drinkable. You need virtually all of any release to be drunk to make what is left collectible!

"As well as our online and telephone business we also get customers through the door and they always ask to see our Ardbegs. I ask them what else they drink and they often say 'I've never tried anything else, I've been told it's the best malt whisky there is.' There is a definite aura about Ardbeg, which is why it does so well. Most Islay fanatics think Ardbeg is the best, so that's how it is!"

Dealing with Ardbeg purchasers and prospective purchasers from many different parts of the world, Sukhinder clearly has a sound sense of who his principal customers are.

"The diehard Ardbeg fanatic is the guy on the street, not the super-rich," he notes. "They have made Ardbeg what it is today. Many new products are made for the moneyed individuals, but they should not forget their diehard customers. I remember that when Glenmorangie released Ardbeg, their five-year forecast for sales was broken in less than half this period. They were very lucky with Ardbeg."

Despite the increasingly deep pockets required by collectors, interest in Ardbeg continues to grow, though most fans can only dream of gathering an array of Ardbegs like those assembled by Geert and Sukhinder. The following pages portray significant bottlings from Geert's remarkable Ardbeg collection.

Key bottlings prior to 1997

	Alc	Size	Age	Year Bottled
Ardbeg Old Islay Malt - Special Liqueur *(page 204)* *bottle with photo of distillery on cream label*	75° Proof	26 FL.OZS	na	c 1970
Ardbeg Old Islay Malt *(page 205)* *Green bottle with illustration on cream label*	80° Proof	26 FL.OZS	na	c 1972
Ardbeg Old Islay Malt - 10-year-old *Green bottle with illustration on cream label*	80° Proof	26 FL.OZS	10	c 1975
Ardbeg - 10-year-old *(page 206)* *Clear bottle with white text on mat black label*	70° Proof	26 FL.OZS	10	Nov 76 - Feb 77
Ardbeg - 10-year-old *(page 207)* *Clear bottle with white and gold text on black label*	70° Proof	75.7cl	10	c 1977/8
Ardbeg - 10-year-old *(page 207)* *Clear bottle with white and gold text on black label*	40%	75cl	10	c1978/9
Ardbeg - 10-year-old *(page 208)* *Green bottle with white and gold text on black label*	40%	75cl	10	c1983/4
Ardbeg - 10-year-old *(page 208)* *Green bottle with white and gold text on black label*	40%	70cl	10	c1983/4
Ardbeg - 15-year-old *(page 209)* *Green bottle with white and gold text on black label*	43%	50cl	15	
Very Old Ardbeg - 30-year-old *(page 209)* *Green bottle with white and gold text on black label*	40%	70cl	30	1996

Bottlings since 1997 (Exc Single Casks)

Aged Releases	Alc	Size	Age	Year Distilled
Ardbeg TEN Years Old	46.0%	70cl	10	
Ardbeg TEN Years Old	46.0%	70cl	10	
Ardbeg TEN Years Old	46.0%	70cl	10	
Ardbeg TEN Years Old	46.0%	750ml	10	
Ardbeg TEN Years Old	46.0%	750ml	10	
Ardbeg TEN Years Old	46.0%	1 liter	10	
Ardbeg TEN Years Old	46.0%	1 liter	10	
Ardbeg TEN Years Old	46.0%	1 liter	10	
Ardbeg TEN Years Old	57.8%	70cl	10	
Ardbeg TEN Years Old	46.0%	70cl	10	
Ardbeg Mor TEN Years Old	57.3%	4500 cl	10	
Ardbeg 17-year-old	40.0%	70cl	17	
Ardbeg 17-year-old	43.0%	1 liter	17	
Ardbeg 17-year-old	43.0%	750ml	17	

Vintages	Alc	Size	Age	Year Distilled
Ardbeg 1990	55.0%	70cl	13	1990
Ardbeg 1990	55.0%	70cl	13	1990
Ardbeg 1978	43.0%	70cl		1978
Ardbeg 1978	43.0%	70cl		1978
Ardbeg 1978	43.0%	70cl		1978
Ardbeg 1978	42.4%	70cl		1978
Ardbeg 1978	43.0%	750ml		1978
Ardbeg 1977	46.0%	70cl	24	1977
Ardbeg 1977	46.0%	70cl	27	1977
Ardbeg 1977	46.0%	750ml	24	1977
Ardbeg 1975	43.0%	70cl		1975
Ardbeg 1975	43.0%	70cl		1975
Ardbeg 1975	43.0%	70cl		1975
Ardbeg 1975	43.0%	70cl		1975
Ardbeg 1965	42.1%	70cl	40	1965

Named Releases	Alc	Size	Age	Year Distilled
Ardbeg Provenance				
Ardbeg Provenance EU	55.6%	70cl	23	1974
Ardbeg Provenance USA 1	54.7%	750ml	24	1974
Ardbeg Provenance USA 2	55.0%	750ml	26	1974
Ardbeg Provenance Asia	55.0%	750ml	26	1974
Ardbeg Provenance	55.0%	750ml	26	1974
Ardbeg Lord of the Isles	46.0%	70cl	25	
Ardbeg Lord of the Isles	46.0%	70cl	25	
Ardbeg Lord of the Isles	46.0%	70cl	25	
Ardbeg Lord of the Isles	46.0%	70cl	25	
Ardbeg Lord of the Isles	46.0%	70cl	25	
Ardbeg Lord of the Isles	46.0%	70cl	25	
Ardbeg Lord of the Isles	46.0%	70cl	25	
Ardbeg Uigeadail	54.2%	70cl		
Ardbeg Uigeadail	54.2%	70cl		1993
Ardbeg Uigeadail	54.2%	70cl		
Ardbeg Uigeadail	54.2%	70cl		
Ardbeg Uigeadail	54.2%	750ml		
Ardbeg Uigeadail	54.2%	750ml		
Ardbeg Uigeadail	54.2%	750ml		
Ardbeg Airigh Nam Beist 1990	46.0%	70cl	16	1990
Ardbeg Airigh Nam Beist 1990	46.0%	70cl	17	1990
Ardbeg Airigh Nam Beist 1990	46.0%	750ml	16	1990
Ardbeg Airigh Nam Beist 1990	46.0%	750ml	17	1990
Ardbeg Very Young	58.3%	70cl	6	1998
Ardbeg Still Young	56.2%	70cl	8	1998
Ardbeg Almost There	54.1%	70cl	9	1998
Ardbeg Renaissance" (We've Arrived!)	55.0%	70cl	10	1998
Ardbeg Double Barrel	49.9%/44.9%	70cl	33	1974
Ardbeg Double Barrel	49.0%/44.3%	70cl	33	1974
Ardbeg Double Barrel	49.0%/47.7%	70cl	33	1974
Ardbeg Double Barrel	49.9%/44.9%	750ml	33	1974

(from 3 pairs of casks, totalling 250 pairs of bottles)

Committee Bottlings	Alc	Size	Age	Year Distilled
Ardbeg 21 years old	56.3%	70cl	21	1979 & 1980
Ardbeg Committee Reserve	55.3%	70cl	28	1974
Very Young Ardbeg Committee Reserve For Discussion	58.9%	70cl	6	1997
Ardbeg Kildalton	57.6%	70cl	24	1980
Ardbeg Committee Reserve Young Uigeadail	59.9%	70cl		

Cask No	Yield	Year Bottled	Bottled For	Comments
		2000		with postal code
				without postal code
			US	introducing ten
			US	introducing ten
				for duty free only
				introducing ten
	/900	2003	Japan	cask strength
				green leather box
	/1000	2007		very large bottle
		1997		
				for duty free
			US (Brown Forman)	
	600	2004		
	1140	2004	Japan	
		1997		
		1998		
		1999		
	/204	1999		
		1998	US (Brown Forman)	
		2001		
		2004		
		2001	US (Brown Forman)	
		1998		
		1999		
		2000		
		2001		
3678 & 3679	/261	2005	World	vatted
	/5000	18 Nov 97	Europe	
	/2500	9 Apr 98	US	
	/2500	21 Sep 00	US	21.09.2000 on front
	/5480 at least	29 Mar 00	Asia	2000 on front label
		21 Sep 00		2000 on front label
		2001		L1
		2002		L2
		2003		L3
		2004		L4
		2005		L5
		2006		L6
		2007		L7
		2003		flip top/white inside
		2004		flip top/black inside
		no date		flip top/black inside
		no date		normal box
			US (Brown Forman)	normal box
			US (Brown Forman)	flip top/white inside
			US (import moet hennessy inc NY)	normal box
		2006		
		2007		
		2006	US	
		2007	US	
		2004		
		2006		
		2007		
		2008		
3145 & 3524		2007	Europe	from 2 single casks
3160 & 3528		2007	UK	from 2 single casks
1745 & 3151		2007	Asia	from 2 single casks
3145 & 3524		2007	US	from 2 single casks
	/2500	2001		from 12 casks
	/3000	2002		
	/4002	2003		
	/1300	2004		
	1392	2006		

Single Cask bottlings since 1997

Single Casks (in order of year released)	Alc	Size	Age	Year Distilled	Cask No	Yield	Year Bottled	Bottled For
First batch including the Managers Choice and two Committee Bottlings								
Ardbeg Manager's Choice *olive lable with Kildalton Cross and black text*	56.0%	70cl	22	24 Nov 1976	2391	/497	23 Jun 1999	
Ardbeg *"black lable, white text. abv in cream box"*	45.2%	70cl	23	26 Dec 1975	4702	/261	20 Oct 1999	France
Ardbeg *brown lable with black text*	46.7%	70cl	23	26 Dec 1975	4718	/238	20 Oct 1999	Italy
Ardbeg Committee *brown lable with black text*	53.2%	70cl	24	24 Nov 1976	2394	/466	16 Jul 2000	
Ardbeg Committee *brown lable with black text*	55.0%	70cl	24	24 Nov 1976	2392	/528	17 Jul 2000	
Ardbeg *olive lable with Kildalton Cross and black text*	46.7%	70cl	24	26 Dec 1975	4700	/248	19 Jul 2000	Japan
Second batch in black cardboard box *(black lable, white text. abv in cream box)*								
Ardbeg	54.5%	70cl	25	24 Nov 1976	2395	/468	26 Mar 2002	Japan
Ardbeg	53.5%	70cl	25	24 Nov 1976	2396	/492	26 Mar 2002	Italy
Ardbeg	44.8%	70cl	26	26 Dec 1975	4716	/228	26 Mar 2002	Germany
Ardbeg	46.2%	70cl	26	26 Dec 1975	4701	/252	26 Mar 2002	France - Societé dugas
Ardbeg	46.2%	70cl	26	26 Dec 1975	4701	/252	26 Mar 2002	France - clan des grands malts
Ardbeg	47.6%	70cl	26	26 Dec 1975	4703	/240	26 Mar 2002	Italy
Ardbeg	53.1%	70cl	25	24 Nov 1976	2390	/494	27 Apr 2002	Islay Festival 02
Ardbeg	44.5%	70cl	28	09 Aug 1974	3475	/126	22 Oct 2002	Oddbins
Ardbeg	49.9%	70cl	31	27 Oct 1972	2782	/246	05 May 2003	Italy
Ardbeg	52.3%	70cl	29	14 Jun 1974	2740	/120	11 Aug 2003	Belgium
Third batch in green presentation box *(black label with gold celtic border)*								
Ardbeg	51.4%	70cl	27	24 Nov 1976	2398	/504	05 May 2004	Islay Festival 04
Ardbeg	48.3%	70cl	32	24 Mar 1972	866	/239	24 Aug 2004	Oddbins
Ardbeg	45.3%	70cl	32	24 Mar 1972	861	/216	13 Oct 2004	Germany
Ardbeg	48.5%	70cl	32	24 Mar 1972	868	/236	13 Oct 2004	Sweden
Ardbeg	49.2%	70cl	31	27 Oct 1972	2781	/216	13 Oct 2004	France
Ardbeg	49.5%	70cl	31	16 Mar 1973	1146	/219	14 Oct 2004	Italy

Single Casks (in order of year released)	Alc	Size	Age	Year Distilled	Cask No	Yield	Year Bottled	Bottled For
Ardbeg	53.7%	70cl	30	14 Jun 1974	2739	/134	14 Oct 2004	Italy
Ardbeg	51.4%	70cl	31	27 Oct 1972	2780	/245	14 Oct 2004	Denmark
Ardbeg	44.2%	70cl	31	10 Nov 1972	3038	/148	14 Oct 2004	Belgium
Ardbeg	49.3%	70cl	31	16 Mar 1973	1143	/216	22 Oct 2004	Distillery
Ardbeg	47.2%	70cl	30	26 Dec 1975	4704	/270	14 Apr 2005	Islay Festival 05
Ardbeg	44.7%	70cl	30	26 Dec 1975	4719	/188	14 Apr 2005	Islay
Ardbeg	53.1%	70cl	31	14 Jun 1974	2738	/75	20 Sep 2005	Belgium
Ardbeg	51.9%	70cl	31	14 Jun 1974	2741	/122	20 Sep 2005	Sweden
Ardbeg (Leather box)	42.7%	70cl	31	14 Jun 1974	2742	/36	20 Sep 2005	Hotels Only
Ardbeg	51.7%	70cl	31	14 Jun 1974	2743	/106	20 Sep 2005	France
Ardbeg	51.0%	70cl	31	14 Jun 1974	2749	/120	20 Sep 2005	Norway
Ardbeg	51.8%	70cl	31	14 Jun 1974	2751	/141	20 Sep 2005	UK
Ardbeg	52.1%	70cl	31	14 Jun 1974	2752	/133	20 Sep 2005	Oddbins
Ardbeg	40.9%	70cl	31	26 Dec 1975	4699	/121	16 Feb 2006	Distillery
Ardbeg	41.4%	70cl	31	26 Dec 1975	4720	/207	16 Feb 2006	Italy
Ardbeg	46.3%	70cl	31	26 Dec 1975	4717	/165	03 May 2006	Islay Festival 06

Fourth batch in black presentation box *(black label with gold celtic border)*

Single Casks	Alc	Size	Age	Year Distilled	Cask No	Yield	Year Bottled	Bottled For
Ardbeg	52.2%	70cl	32	12 Jul 1974	3306	/126	31 Aug 2006	Denmark
Ardbeg	52.5%	70cl	32	12 Jul 1974	3309	/109	31 Aug 2006	France
Ardbeg	54.5%	70cl	32	12 Jul 1974	3326	/110	23 Sep 2006	Germany
Ardbeg	54.1%	70cl	32	12 Jul 1974	3327	/117	25 Sep 2006	Italy
Ardbeg	53.5%	70cl	32	12 Jul 1974	3328	/76	25 Sep 2006	Italy
Ardbeg	48.0%	70cl	31	04 Oct 1974	4547	/133	25 Sep 2006	Sweden
Ardbeg	46.7%	70cl	31	25 Oct 1974	4985	/93	25 Sep 2006	UK
Ardbeg	50.7%	70cl	31	25 Oct 1974	4989	/132	25 Sep 2006	UK
Ardbeg	51.8%	70cl	31	22 Nov 1974	5666	/168	25 Sep 2006	UK
Ardbeg	53.9%	70cl	32	12 Jul 1974	3324	/118	26 Sep 2006	Belgium
Ardbeg	54.2%	70cl	31	28 Mar 1975	1375	/522	08 Nov 2006	Distillery
Ardbeg	53.7%	70cl	31	28 Mar 1975	1378	/453	08 Nov 2006	World
Ardbeg	52.8%	70cl	17	30 Aug 1990	86	/300	11 Apr 2007	Fortnum & Masons

Ardbeg Old Islay Malt – Special Liqueur, bottled at 75° proof

26⅔ FL.OZS.　　　　　　　　80° PROOF

ARDBEG

OLD ISLAY MALT
SCOTCH WHISKY
ARDBEG DISTILLERY LIMITED
ISLAY

Ardbeg 10-year-old at 70° proof (mat label)

Four slightly different bottles of Ardbeg 10-year-old, one at 75cl, two at 70cl and one with no stated capacity at all

Ardbeg 15-year-old, 50cl at 43% ABV and Very Old Ardbeg 30-year-old at 40% ABV

ESTABLISHED 1815

Very Old

Ardbeg

FINEST
ISLAY SINGLE MALT
SCOTCH WHISKY

Guaranteed **30** years old

ARDBEG DISTILLERY LIMITED
ISLE OF ISLAY ARGYLL SCOTLAND

70cl ℮   L01655   40% Vol

ESTABLISHED 1815

Ardbeg

FINEST
ISLAY SINGLE MALT
SCOTCH WHISKY

Guaranteed **15** years old

ARDBEG DISTILLERY LIMITED
ISLE OF ISLAY ARGYLL SCOTLAND

50cl ℮   L01473   43% Vol

Ten Ardbeg Single Cask
bottlings from 2nd batch

The range of Ardbeg miniatures,
first introduced in 1976

Our sincere thanks go to the following people for their invaluable time, interest and support:

Former Employees
Hamish Scott
Ian Miller
Alastair Cunningham
Robert Hicks
John Black
Iain Henderson
Duncan Logan
Ed Dodson
Stuart Thomson

Current Employees
Hamish Torrie
Dr Bill Lumsden
Michael Heads
Jackie Thomson
Emma McGechie
Alistair Blair
Douglas Bowman ('Dugga')
James Gillespie ('The Gow')
Alastair Johnston ('Asha')
Neil Johnston ('Philco')
Alec Livingstone ('Azza')
Ruaraidh Macintyre ('Mackie')
Archie McKechnie ('Yogi')

Andrew Mullen ('Drew')
Malcolm Rennie
Alexander Woodrow, ('Wardie')

Others
Alastair Lawson
Dorothy Dennis
Mark Reynier
Christine McCafferty
- Diageo Archive Manager
Ian Russell
- Archivist Glasgow University
Eddie Brown
David Adams
Donnie McKinnon
Han Van Wees
Sukhinder Singh
Geert Bero
Bert Vuik
Ingvar Andersson
Jarkko Nikkanen
Jorgen Andersson
Rhona Scott

Time for a dram!